PENGUIN ANANDA

THE ART AND SCIENCE OF HAPPINESS

Swami Mukundananda is a world-renowned spiritual teacher from India and an international authority on mind management. He earned his degrees from the prestigious IIT Delhi and IIM Calcutta. He worked with a multinational firm for a short while, then renounced a promising career to enter monkhood. He studied Vedic scriptures at the feet of Jagadguru Kripaluji Maharaj. For almost four decades now, Swami Mukundananda has been sharing his vast knowledge through his books, lectures and life-transformation programmes.

Swamiji meets hundreds, even thousands, of people every day from all walks of life. His steadfast positivity exudes hope, clarity and a sense of purpose for those who connect with him. He has deeply affected the lives of millions of people who have been drawn to his profound integrity, charismatic personality and passion to serve. Those who meet him experience his warmth and compassion, and also feel deeply touched by him. Swamiji's lectures are humorous, his arguments logical and well laid out, and most of all, his advice is practical. His lectures on social media platforms are loved and followed by millions. Swamiji divides his time between India and the US.

T0124150

Celebrating 35 Years of
Penguin Random House India

The ART & SCIENCE *of* HAPPINESS

SWAMI MUKUNDANANDA

Bestselling author of *The Power of Thoughts*

PENGUIN
ANANDA

An imprint of Penguin Random House

PENGUIN ANANDA

USA | Canada | UK | Ireland | Australia
New Zealand | India | South Africa | China

Penguin Ananda is part of the Penguin Random House group of companies
whose addresses can be found at global.penguinrandomhouse.com

Published by Penguin Random House India Pvt. Ltd
4th Floor, Capital Tower 1, MG Road,
Gurugram 122 002, Haryana, India

First published in Penguin Ananda by Penguin Random House India 2023

10 9 8 7 6 5 4 3 2 1

ISBN 9780143452348

Typeset in Sabon by Manipal Technologies Limited, Manipal

www.penguin.co.in

This book is dedicated to my beloved Spiritual Master, Jagadguru Shree Kripaluji Maharaj, the embodiment of divine love and grace, who illuminated humankind with the purest rays of divine knowledge. He was immersed in the highest bliss of divine love and engaged in inundating the entire planet with it. I am eternally indebted to him for bestowing upon me his divine wisdom and for inspiring me to consecrate my life to its propagation. I pray that by his blessings this book will help sincere seekers find everlasting happiness.

Contents

Introduction

Happiness is the experience of feeling joy and well-being. Being happy brings a smile to the face and contentment to the heart. It gives us peace and makes life worthwhile. Desiring happiness is at the core of our being. It is the driving force behind all our actions. That is why all of us, irrespective of our education and profession, pursue it in all we do.

However, simply seeking happiness does not miraculously put it in our lap. It is something we must generate within ourselves. After all, we all have attained a certain amount of success, yet we remain unsatiated. Sadly, we ourselves undermine our joy by negative emotions, while ignoring the abundance in our lives.

But what if I said that you can learn to create happiness? Yes, that's right. Just as we have learnt to produce thoughts and behaviours that make us miserable, we can also learn the art and science of being happy. Imagine joy that does not depend on externals; joy that is not fleeting; and joy that grows forever. While this may sound impossible or like a fairy tale, this is true happiness as explained in all the scriptures. It can withstand the harshest of conditions and make you feel on top of the world—always.

So, the golden question is: 'How do we learn the art of being happy?' We all have the power to control our thoughts, behaviours, relationships and habits, and direct our life towards happier living. It comes down to the attitudes and perspectives that we harbour in situations and relationships. And if we take it a step further, it comes from our connection with the Divine, which enlivens our spirit and situates us in eternal bliss.

The most important factor that determines whether we find happiness is where we search for it. There are different kinds of happiness. The spectrum ranges from the mere thrill of sense gratification to the most fulfilling supreme divine bliss. Our misery stems from the fact that we chase the wrong kind of happiness. If we can learn what will give us true happiness and where to find it, we will be well on our way to achieving it.

That is the aim of this book—to equip you with insights and wisdom that will ensure you choose wisely and set yourself on the path to master the art and science of happiness. We will learn the wisdom to cultivate happiness in our everyday life. We will identify best practices and principles that will enable you to be cheerful and in high spirits no matter what.

In this book, I have addressed happiness from various dimensions. The subject is vast, but for the sake of conciseness, I have covered topics that are most relevant to all. A chapter is included on the neurology of happiness, which reveals lifestyle habits that evoke happy hormones in the brain. This science-backed knowledge gives you the tools to induce happiness through thoughts and actions.

Further, a chapter is dedicated to one of the most transformative tools for being joyful—positive reframing. This means changing our perspective to see the silver lining in difficult situations. As the saying goes in Hindi: *drishti badalne se srishti badaltī hai*— 'When you change how you look at things, the world changes for you.'

Expanding on the technique of reframing, there is a practical chapter on how to be happy in the face of adversity. We all realize that adversity is an inevitable part of life. If we want to insulate ourselves from the vagaries of life, we must learn how to handle difficulties without losing our mental peace. This chapter presents techniques for converting obstacles into opportunities and growing our inner strength.

Our relationships are one of the greatest sources of happiness. We all crave genuine love and authentic heart-to-heart connections with others. This is why there is a chapter dedicated to cultivating strong and beautiful relationships in our lives. You will learn how to reduce expectations, practise selfless love and diminish strife in your dealings.

Living for a higher purpose is probably the most satisfying feeling. Where money and power fail to bring contentment, a sense of purpose exhilarates us with euphoric fulfilment. To that end, you will find an illuminating chapter on how to pursue meaningful goals and discover a sense of purpose that deeply gratifies you. Similarly, there is a revealing chapter on how to be happy at the workplace by learning about the concept of 'flow'. In it, you will discover timeless wisdom to working stress-free.

Since the subject of happiness has intrigued many philosophers through the ages, there is an interesting chapter on the prominent teachings of thought leaders in history. We conclude the book with the Vedic perspective on happiness and top it off with the ultimate source of happiness and how to reach it. Further, the book includes a heart-warming chapter on how generosity multiplies our happiness.

This book is meant to serve as a comprehensive teaching on how to be happy in every aspect of life and in any situation. I have explained the art of happiness pragmatically and scientifically, with hands-on applications, real-life stories and anecdotes to bring forth the ideas. Every chapter is replete with wisdom to enrich your intellect. The subject matter is further embellished with tools you can use right away to become happier.

My best wishes to you on the journey to true happiness and bliss that, once achieved, will forever stay with you.

Swami Mukundananda

1

The Search for Happiness

Happiness is such an exhilarating feeling. It fills our heart with emotions of positivity, hope and optimism. Happy people feel satisfied with their lives and naturally fulfilled at work. Gratitude grows easily in them, leading to a deep sense of well-being. Every so often, that scales up to the state of euphoria.

Without happiness, success provides no relish. The world's finest luxuries do not fill the void in our heart, and even victory is not sweet. Happiness is thus the 'one' before all the 'zeros'. It multiplies the value of everything by its presence. But it also nullifies the biggest triumphs by its absence.

Ironically, this beautiful feeling called 'happiness' is also the most elusive. We search for it in corporate boardrooms, discotheques, relationships and vacations. But like the lovely rainbow on the horizon, it keeps receding mysteriously. Even after running behind it all our lives, our soul informs us from within, 'I have not yet found the joy I seek.'

When did our quest for happiness begin? Let us find out.

'Give Me Happiness'

The first thing we did after birth was to scream, 'I want happiness.' Well, not in those exact words since we had not yet learnt to talk, but what we did amounted to it.

The moment we entered this world, we cried. Why? Because in the process of birth, we experienced pain. By wailing in agony, we expressed the deepest sentiment of our being. 'I have not come into this world for misery. I have come for joy. Waa . . .! Waa . . .! Waa . . .! Give me happiness!'

Since then, we have been in constant pursuit of it. Our quest takes on a variety of forms. Mahesh runs after wealth, while Dinesh goes after power and prestige. Meena focuses on relationships, while Bina is convinced earning a PhD is the most desirable thing.

munde munde matirbhinnaḥ kunde kunde navaṁ payaḥ
(Vāyu Puran)

'Just as water differs from lake to lake, so also the thoughts in our head differ from person to person.' Likewise, we all differ in our desires too.

Our goals seem much different, but factually, we all are searching for the same one thing—happiness—as the following conversation illustrates.

Ask Mahesh, whom we met three paragraphs above, 'Why do you want wealth?'

'With money, I will get the things of the world,' he responds.

Ask him again, 'Why do you want the things of the world?'

'I will be able to take care of my family,' he replies.

Ask him yet again, 'Why do you wish to take care of your family?'

'It will make me happy,' he answers.

The chain of Mahesh's responses ended in happiness. All his desires and goals are in pursuit of it.

Now ask the others—Dinesh, Meena and Bina— the same chain of questions. 'What do you want?' Whatever they respond, again ask, 'Why do you want that?' And so on.

In each instance, the final answer will be, 'It will make me happy.'

For everyone on the planet, the concluding answer will always be, 'It will make me happy.' This means all of us, without exception, have one final goal—to be blissful.

Aristotle, who lived 2500 years ago, was aware of this principle underlying all human behaviour. He wrote:

> We choose honour, wealth and prestige because they give us happiness. But we choose happiness for itself and never with a view for anything further.

It may have astonished Aristotle to know that 2500 years prior to him, Ved Vyas, the writer of eighteen Puranas, had made the same observation:

> *sarveshām-api bhūtānāṁ nṛipa svātmaiva vallabhaḥ*
> *itare 'patya-vittādhyās-tad-vallabha-tayaiva hi*
> (Bhagavatam 10.14.50)

'Everyone loves their own happiness. If they seem to love anything else—children, wealth and the like—it is because they believe these will bring them joy.'

Who Taught Us to Desire Happiness?

Is it not astonishing? We are eight billion humans on the planet. We all differ from each other in many ways. Our facial appearances are different. Our biometrics do not match. Our voices have a unique mix of octaves. Even our bodily aromas are different, which is easily picked up by dogs.

Likewise, with regard to happiness too, we should have had varied tastes: Someone desires unadulterated happiness, another wants pure misery, while a third yearns for a fifty-fifty mix of joy and distress. However, when it comes to joy, we all are alike. We all want happiness alone.

Did anyone teach us in childhood to pursue bliss? Just as our parents and teachers instructed us, 'My son! You should never steal.' or 'My daughter! You should always tell the truth.' Similarly, did anyone train us: 'My child! You must make happiness your goal. It must not come about that you start running after misery.'

No! We were never trained to seek happiness, which is even more astonishing because we had to be taught everything else. We had to be tutored regarding the number system, addition and subtraction. We did not learn the alphabet by ourselves. In fact, we required guidance even to recognize our mother. People around us kept urging, 'She is your mother, say, "Mummy".' Finally, we took the cue and began saying, 'Mummy'.

Everything was taught but the pursuit of happiness was not. It came naturally to us. Mysterious, isn't it?

Our Contradictory Desires

The mystery of happiness deepens on realizing that in its pursuit, we do contradictory things. Sometimes, we love company, and other times, we prefer isolation.

On occasion, we prefer the outdoors, while at other times, we choose the indoors. These are mutually opposite activities, but we pursue them all with the same unwavering intention of joy. Let me share my own experience of it.

I often ask people sitting in my discourses, 'Are you enjoying the talk?'

Some respond, 'Yes, Swamiji! Very much.'

I again ask them, 'If I keep speaking for the next four hours, will you continue to sit?'

They reply, 'No, we will get up and leave.'

'Why?' I question again. 'You said that the lecture is enjoyable.'

'That is right, Swamiji,' they respond. 'But after listening for four hours, going away will give us happiness.'

Isn't this so interesting? They choose to sit and enjoy the programme. It gives them pleasure. But when the joy dries up, they prefer to leave, again for the sake of pleasure. The activity reverses, yet the goal—happiness—remains the same.

Sometimes, we decide to sleep because it will provide rest and make us happy. At other times, we choose to be awake because sleeping seems boring. The activity reverses, but the goal of seeking joy remains the same.

Now, a big surprise—we even cry because we find happiness in it. Generally, people believe that laughing is a pleasurable activity while crying is a miserable one. But the Vedas inform us that we even weep for happiness. When our experience of misery crosses our tolerance limit, we begin to cry. It helps us release our pent-up emotions, and this provides a sense of relief. If, instead, crying was truly a painful activity, why would we engage in it?

In conclusion, since the time we were born till today, all we have done has been in search of happiness. Twenty-four hours a day, we have been incessantly looking for it.

And now, an even bigger surprise. This quest for bliss is not of one lifetime—it has been continuing from innumerable past lives. As per the Vedas, just as God has no beginning, likewise, our soul too is beginningless, endless and eternal. The *Shwetāshvatar Upanishad* states:

jñājñau dvāv-ajā-vīshanīshā-vajā
hyekā bhoktṛi-bhogyārtha-yuktā   (mantra 1.9)

'Two entities are unborn: One is omniscient, the other is ignorant. One is all-powerful, the other helpless. There is yet another entity, maya, that is also unborn. It has entangled the soul in enjoying the objects of the senses.'

Hence, the present life is not our first. We are eternal, like God. Consider this illustrative example.

I once asked a little girl, 'Where is your father's house?'

She responded sweetly, 'Swamiji, it is in front of my uncle's house.'

I then questioned her, 'Where is your uncle's house?'

She replied, 'It is in front of my father's house.'

'But where are both your father's and uncle's houses?' I inquired.

She responded, 'They are in front of each other.'

Similarly, since when have we existed? Ever since God has existed.

Since when has God existed? Ever since the soul has existed.

Since when have we and God both existed? When even time did not exist, since then.

akṣharāt saṅjāyate kālaḥ (*Shiv Athvarvashirsha*)

Time begins after creation. During maha pralaya (dissolution), there is no time. The soul, therefore, existed even before time started. Our quest for divine bliss, therefore, is of innumerable lifetimes. Why is it that after relentlessly pursuing it since eternity, the attainment of perfect joy still remains so elusive?

The Happiness Riddle

The world abounds with stories of people who dreamed of amassing wealth, fame and power. After years of struggle, they succeeded in materializing those dreams. And yet, they discovered their lives were still empty, and they were devoid of happiness. A classic example is Oscar Wilde.

Oscar Wilde was a playwright, poet, novelist and critic. He is remembered in history as a man of unlimited potential. Born in 1854, he received his education in Britain's best schools, winning scholarships all the way through. He was honoured as 'First in Greats' at Oxford and was awarded the Newdigate Prize for poetry.

Oscar Wilde's talent seemed limitless. His plays were popular, earning him lots of money, and he was the toast of London. The *British Heritage* magazine called him 'our most quotable writer' after Shakespeare. Yet at the time of death, he was broken and miserable. He wrote about his life:

> I must say to myself that I ruined myself, and that nobody great or small can be ruined except by his own hand. I am quite ready to say so. Terrible as was what the world did to me, what I did to myself was far more terrible still.

If happiness had a price, the wealthy would be the first to buy it. If it could be manufactured in factories, industrialists would have been the happiest people. If it could be grown in gardens, farmers would have reaped it in harvest. Unfortunately, none of these are possible.

Happiness cannot be purchased at a five-star mall, nor is it a gift that the postman can deliver to our mailbox. The testimony of John D. Rockefeller, the wealthiest American in modern history, revealed this pitiable state on his deathbed. He admitted, 'I have made many millions, but they have brought me no happiness.'[1]

Was Rockefeller not seeking happiness in his life? Yes he was, but the pleasure he got did not satisfy him. People do not reject pleasure because they dislike it. Rather, they discover it has painful consequences. Then the realization dawns that they do not know how to pursue happiness. Though becoming joyful is their goal, the best strategy for achieving it remains a mystery.

Finding joy is the most important art to master in life and the most valuable science to understand. Let us learn it step-by-step as we go through the chapters of this book.

---

[1] John D. Rockefeller, Quotetab, https://www.quotetab.com/quote/by-john-d-rockefeller/i-have-made-many-millions-but-they-have-brought-me-no-happiness.

Summary

- We all seek happiness. It is the most exhilarating feeling.

- We have been in constant pursuit of happiness since birth. All our desires and goals are oriented towards the attainment of happiness.

- The journey of our soul did not begin in this life. We are eternal, like God. Therefore, this quest for bliss is not of one lifetime; it has been continuing from innumerable past lives.

- After relentlessly pursuing happiness for endless lives, the attainment of perfect joy remains elusive.

2

Benefits of Happiness

In the previous chapter, we learnt how happiness adds joy and brightness to life. Not only do people want to be blissful, but they also want to increase their happiness quotient to the level of euphoria. And rightly so. The quality of our life experience is intricately linked to joy. Blissfulness makes life worthwhile. But what are the tools and techniques for enhancing our happiness? And where do we begin the journey?

As a first step, we must know the manifold benefits of a happier state of mind. This will deepen our motivation to master the art and science of happiness. Therefore, in this chapter, we shall start by looking at the numerous tangible benefits of joy.

Happiness Can Boost Your Immunity

Today, science and research endorse that psychology can alter physiology. Anger can raise your blood pressure and send your heart racing. Tension can drive away sleep; it can lead to digestive problems and cause aches and pains in the body. Likewise, the immune system's antibody response to pathogens is also affected by moods.

People's emotional status and its correlation to immunity was the subject of a study by Sheldon Cohen and his colleagues of Carnegie Mellon University.[1]

The experiment involved 334 healthy volunteers. Prior to the trial, they were evaluated on their emotional states. Participants were assessed on their proclivity towards positive emotions, such as happiness and contentment, versus negative emotions, such as anxiety and depression.

Subsequently, they were given nasal drops of rhinovirus (the germ that causes colds). Their saliva was then tested for antibodies. The same participants were tested week after week. The findings revealed that on days they were happier, their antibody response was much stronger. And vice versa. Being joyful had a protective effect on the body.

A high antibody response indicates a robust immune system, ready to defend against invaders. So, yes, being

---

[1] A. Palmer, 'Positive Emotion Styles Linked to the Common Cold', *American Psychological Association*, November 2003, https://www.apa.org/monitor/nov03/positive.

happy can improve your immunity and help you stay healthy. One more reason to harbour positive thoughts and feelings!

On the other hand, a negative mood can suppress parts of the immune system and make you prone to a variety of ailments. Being blissful, therefore, is a 'must have' for good health.

Happiness Can Protect Your Heart

Anxiety puts extra strain on the heart. It can cause the heart to race, leaving the blood speeding through the veins and the lungs gasping for more air. However, the body is not equipped to deal with this for long.

Consequently, after any stressful event, the body seeks to return to its resting equilibrium as soon as possible. The heart, especially, is not designed to beat quickly for long periods of time. Tension undermines it by prolonging the state of overwork. The resultant wear and tear from sustained anxiety increases the risk of heart attacks. Instead, a blissful mood leads to a healthier heart.

Happiness Can Help Fight Stress

Uncertainty and stressful situations are an inevitable part of life. Pleasure and sorrow enter our lives at regular intervals like the summer and winter seasons.

Hence, the ability to deal with stressful situations is a key component to a good life. And a happy disposition empowers us to better cope with all kinds of challenges. How is that?

Well, managing stress is an art. Happy individuals master it by simply changing their perception of the event. Rather than viewing it as a calamity, they choose to see the inherent opportunity in it for growth.

In fact, this is exactly what happens. After dealing with the stressor, our brain starts rewiring itself to remember and learn from the experience. It self-programmes to deal with similar stressors more effectively in future.

Conversely, negative emotions get us into trouble. Too much worry about the future or rumination over the past distract us from giving our best. It leads to tunnel vision, in which the mind gets fixated on negative circumstances to the exclusion of all the positives around.

People who view stress as harmful tend to resort to harmful coping mechanisms such as drinking, procrastinating or catastrophizing. In contrast, those who view stress positively thrive by seeking support, learning a lesson, finding a solution or simply not concerning themselves with adverse things.

Thus, those who are emotionally sound are more resilient to stress. Such small shifts in our thoughts make a huge difference to our life experience. Yet another benefit of happiness and reason to be happy!

Happiness Promotes a Healthy Lifestyle

We naturally feel upbeat when we eat healthy, exercise regularly and sleep well. But it works the other way around too. Being happy can motivate us to follow a healthy lifestyle. What are the healthy habits that joyous people tend to adopt?

The mind and body both impact each other. The food people eat influences their nature. And the reverse—those with pure mind prefer pure foods—is also true. They gravitate towards a sattvic diet (foods in the mode of goodness).

Great luminaries such as Mahatma Gandhi, Bertrand Russel, Leo Tolstoy, Leonardo da Vinci, Pythagoras, George Bernard Shaw, Thomas Edison and Benjamin Franklin—all had one thing in common. They were vegetarian. Their sattvic thoughts naturally made food conducive to high thinking attractive to them. The Bhagavad Gita says:

āyuḥ-sattva-balārogya-sukha-prīti-vivardhanāḥ
rasyāḥ snigdhāḥ sthirā hṛidyā āhārāḥ sāttvika-priyāḥ
(verse 17.8)

'Persons in the mode of goodness prefer foods that promote lifespan and increase virtue, strength, health, happiness and satisfaction. Such foods are juicy, succulent, nourishing and naturally tasteful.'

Similarly, a positive attitude motivates people to engage in more physical activity. Regular movement and exercise promote well-being. They help build strong bones, decrease fat and lower blood pressure. That is why children imbued with emotions of joy venture outdoors—they run around, swing on branches and play with friends. Likewise, happy people are more active and healthier.

Let us not forget about sleep. It too improves with a positive mindset. Too much excitement can lead to poor sleep. After all, too much of a good thing is bad. Positive feelings help us sleep soundly.

Interestingly, harbouring positivity has a compounded multiplier effect on good habits. Let me illustrate through a compelling study done by American psychologists Ellen Langer and Alia Crum.[2]

The study involved an experiment on eighty-four housekeepers across several hotels. The participants were measured on health markers such as weight, Body Mass Index (BMI) and blood pressure. At the start of the experiment, the maids were informed of

---

[2] Newsweek Staff, 'Placebo Power: Can 'Thinking' Fit Get You Fit?', *Newsweek*, 26 February 2007, https://www.newsweek.com/placebo-power-can-thinking-fit-get-you-fit-104985.

the health benefits of exercise. They were then asked whether they were exercising. The maids' response was that they did not have the time for it.

Subsequently, half the maids were tutored on how their work—cleaning, making beds, vacuuming—provided sufficient exercise to keep fit. They were even told the number of calories burned per activity. The other half of the cleaning staff were not told the health benefits of their job.

The psychologists returned three months later and repeated the physical exams. The findings were clear. The informed housekeepers—perceiving exercise benefits in their work—had lost weight, improved BMI and lowered cholesterol levels. They even reported liking their job more. In sharp contrast, the uninformed maids reported no such health benefits.

The study indicates how a positive attitude improves the reality we live in, thus adding value to our work.

What about social habits? As you may have guessed, happier people are more inclined to wear seatbelts, spend mindfully and contribute positively to society. They volunteer more for social causes and are responsible members of society. They are more likely to vote and have respect for law and order.

As we can see, being happy makes us choose wisely and behave correctly. The outcome is better lifestyle habits, constructive outcomes and a healthier you!

Will happiness help you live a longer life? It turns out the answer is 'Yes!' as we shall see next.

Happiness Can Increase Your Lifespan

As discussed, happiness helps us build physical and mental resources. Good health and inner joy enable us to live longer as evidenced by a landmark study on Catholic nuns.[3]

One hundred and eighty nuns of the School Sisters of Notre Dame, born before 1917, maintained autobiographical journals. Recently, researchers obtained access to their diaries, based on which they evaluated how happy the nuns were. They also noted how long the nuns had lived.

The results were revealing. Ninety per cent of the happiest quartile of nuns had survived beyond the age of eighty-five, whereas only 34 per cent of the least happy quartile had lived to that age.

We can safely conclude that positive emotions enhance the duration of life. But it does not stop there. One substantial study by the longest-serving professor of psychology at Harvard, Ellen Langer, showed how age is just a number.

---

[3] Elizabeth Scott, 'The Link Between Happiness and Health', Verywell Mind, 17 March 2020, https://www.verywellmind.com/the-link-between-happiness-and-health-3144619.

Losing your hair, mental decline, lack of personal control and being weak are attributes stereotyped for ageing. However, we all age differently—some gracefully while others miserably. Why is that? The ageing process is directly influenced by the way we perceive ourselves.

In 1979, Langer experimented on a group of seventy-five-year-old men for roughly a week.[4] The men were oblivious to the nature of the study. They were invited to a free retreat, but not permitted to bring newspapers, books or pictures dated after 1959.

At the retreat, time was turned back to 1959 when these men were fifty-five years old. They noticed black and white TVs, magazines from that era and a vintage radio—all designed to take them back to the 'good old times' when they were younger and fitter. The participants were also asked to dress as per the fashion of 1959 and act the way they did twenty years prior. They were directed to converse about events pertaining to that time in their lives.

These seventy-five-year-old men were now behaving and feeling like fifty-five-year-olds. The idea was to prove the strong association between the mind and the

---

[4] Bruce Grierson, 'What if Age Is Nothing but a Mind-Set?', *The New York Times Magazine*, 22 October 2014, https://www.nytimes.com/2014/10/26/magazine/what-if-age-is-nothing-but-a-mind-set.html.

body. Can tweaking subjective reality change objective reality?

The men's biomarkers such as hand grip, flexibility, hearing, vision and memory were assessed before and after the retreat. The results proved Langer's hypothesis. After the retreat, most men were more supple, held better posture and could grip stronger than before. An improvement in eyesight and memory was also observed. And guess what? The men looked three years younger on average than when they arrived.

Again, this brings us back to how thoughts impact our well-being. Being optimistic is important to vigour and vitality; positivity can create a healthier you! So, if you want to stay fit and live long, cultivate joyful thoughts.

You will find the next section especially interesting. It will show how positive beliefs are naturally healing for the body.

Placebo Effect—Mind over Matter Healing

The placebo effect is a fascinating phenomenon in which psychology meets human biology. It occurs when people experience real physiological benefits from fake treatment. They believe they are receiving the medicine, while they are actually administered a blank sugar pill, i.e., a placebo. Yet, they show marked improvement in symptoms.

In fact, double-blind placebo trials are considered the gold standard for approval of new medication in medical research. In clinical trials, both doctors and patients are not privy to who is taking the active drug versus the placebo pill.

If the volunteers taking the real drug report marked improvement over those taking the placebo, the drug passes the test. Surprisingly, this number is hovering only around 10 per cent.[5] This means only 10 per cent of new drugs surpass the placebo's curative impact. This proves that the placebo response is very real. The body has natural healing abilities. And when you add to that a positive mindset, together they prime the body to cure itself.

The mind-body mechanism has a symbiotic relationship. Our thoughts can cause physiological changes. Hence, our mindsets and beliefs can work as medicine. They can trigger recuperative responses from the immune, endocrine and cardiovascular systems. This is not to discredit medical treatment but rather to highlight the power of the natural healing that is activated by our mindsets.

Consider the example of arthroscopic surgery, which is common for osteoarthritis of the knee. Symptoms

[5] Brian Resnick, 'The Weird Power of the Placebo Effect, Explained', Vox, 7 July 2017, https://www.vox.com/science-and-health/2017/7/7/15792188/placebo-effect-explained.

of osteoarthritis include pain, swelling and stiffness in the knee joint. In arthroscopic surgery, incisions are made around the knee and instruments are inserted. The condition of the knee is then assessed, and one of three alternatives are employed. Either 1) the joint is scraped clean of debris; or 2) the knee is cleaned with water; or 3) nothing is done, and the incision is merely stitched up.

Dr Bruce Moseley of Baylor College of Medicine in Houston compared the placebo effect with this popular surgical procedure.[6] The study consisted of 180 patients that were randomly divided into three groups. For the first group, worn cartilage was removed. For the second group, bad cartilage was flushed out. For the third group, nothing was done. Yet, surprisingly, this group experienced the same amount of pain relief and ability to function as those who had the real surgeries.

This is the power of beliefs! We can make our mindsets work in our favour to become healthier. The placebo effect has especially proven efficacious in conditions such as depression, pain management, phobias, asthma and side effects of cancer, such as fatigue.

---

[6] Baylor College of Medicine, 'Study Finds Common Knee Surgery No Better Than Placebo', *ScienceDaily*, 12 July 2002, https://www.sciencedaily.com/releases/2002/07/020712075415.htm.

The placebo response is not magic; there is a reason why it works. Numerous factors contribute to this psychological phenomenon. One of them is the hormone response—the release of healing neurotransmitters. The second is expectations—the brain fires neurons based on what it believes will happen. Though simple enough, these are powerful because they harness the power of the mind. Let us look at both.

1. Hormone Response

Our body is beautifully equipped to heal. It fights cancer cells daily. It defends against infections regularly. It expels unwanted toxins, which would otherwise be harmful. The body's self-repair mechanisms are always working in our favour. However, they operate better when we are relaxed versus stressed.

Stress triggers the release of cortisol and epinephrine, causing the 'fight or flight response'. The body gears up to either fight a threat or flee it. It is driven by our Sympathetic Nervous System (SNS) which energizes and stimulates the body. When SNS is in high gear, the heart starts beating faster, blood pressure rises and blood flow reduces to the organs and increases to the muscles.

In contrast, the relaxation response triggers our ParaSympathetic Nervous System (PSNS). This slows down our heart rate and breathing, lowers blood pressure and aids digestion. It also releases hormones that heal, such as serotonin, nitric oxide and endorphins. In this state, healing occurs, such as cellular regeneration and detoxification. The more time we spend in the relaxed PSNS state, the greater the healing. Thus, the more the mind is at peace, the healthier we will be.

In a placebo response, when we believe that a drug will work and is delivered by a caring healthcare professional, the brain taps into the PSNS. It activates the release of neurotransmitters that are therapeutic. That is why medical science has realized that placebos are 55–60 per cent as effective as most pain medications![7]

2. Expectancy Theory

One of the mechanisms by which the placebo effect works is through expectations. If you expect to get better, your body will work towards it and make you better. Assurance that you are receiving a suitable drug could create the expectations. They could also

---

[7] Sandra Blakeslee, 'Placebos Prove So Powerful Even Experts Are Surprised; New Studies Explore the Brain's Triumph Over Reality', *The New York Times*, 13 October 1998, https://www.nytimes.com/1998/10/13/science/placebos-prove-so-powerful-even-experts-are-surprised-new-studies-explore-brain.html.

arise from the spoken words of a doctor or nurse. Or even from the simple act of taking a pill. For example, you could be feeling good because the doctor claimed the medicine will heal you, or because you were administered an appropriate drug that would heal or simply because you find the doctor's bedside manner and tone reassuring.

How does what we expect actually affect what happens? Expectation of a particular outcome triggers the brain's neurons to fire as if it was actually happening. This activates the nervous system, resulting in real physiological and cognitive consequences. Thus, if you are expecting a result, the brain will respond in a way that enables the outcome. This is also called the 'Expectancy Theory' by psychologists.

Dr Fabrizio Benedetti and colleagues conducted an interesting placebo study that proves the association between expectations and the healing of the body.[8]

The researchers monitored a group of patients undergoing thoracic surgery. Due to its invasiveness, the procedure is painful. It requires slitting the muscles of the side and back to reach the heart and lungs. Soon after the anaesthesia fades away, the patients are given high doses of morphine to counteract the pain.

---

[8] YT, TEDx Talks, Dr Alia Crum, 'Change Your Mindset, Change the Game', TEDxTraverseCity, 15 October 2014, https://www.youtube.com/watch?v=0tqq66zwa7g. Accessed 30 September 2022.

Dr Benedetti slightly modified this routine treatment. Half of the patients were administered morphine by a doctor. The other half were given the same dose of morphine, but through a pre-programmed pump into their IV, so they were unaware of it.

The results showed patients receiving morphine from the doctor experienced significantly more pain relief than those who received it via IV. What happened here? Though morphine was acting directly on neurochemical receptors in the brain, its analgesic powers grew when the patients knew they were receiving a painkiller and that too from a caring professional.

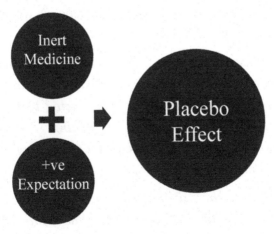

Figure 1: Positive Expectations Lead to Placebo Effect

Fascinated by the results, Dr Benedetti carried out similar experiments to test the efficacy of treatments for hypertension, anxiety and Parkinson's disease. The results remarkably pointed to the same conclusion. When patients were aware of the treatment and expected to benefit from it, they did. However, those who were unaware they were receiving treatment did not benefit to the same degree.

Hence, our expectation to heal puts into motion the body's healing forces and mechanisms.

Nocebo Effect—Harmless Turns into Harmful

Expectations can work the other way around as well and harm the body. This is known as the nocebo effect and is the reverse of the placebo. A well-known Japanese experiment illustrates this concept.[9]

Thirteen participants were blindfolded and informed that one arm was being rubbed with poison ivy. Interestingly, all thirteen people reacted to the plant, exhibiting symptoms of rash, itching, redness and boils. However, the plant was not poison ivy, but just a harmless shrub.

The researchers then rubbed the actual poison ivy on the other arm of the participants while mentioning that

[9] Sandra Blakeslee, 'Placebos Prove So Powerful Even Experts Are Surprised; New Studies Explore the Brain's Triumph Over Reality', *The New York Times*, 13 October 1998, https://www.nytimes.com/1998/10/13/science/placebos-prove-so-powerful-even-experts-are-surprised-new-studies-explore-brain.html.

the plant was inert and harmless. I am sure by now you can guess what happened. Only two people developed adverse symptoms.

Such is the power of negative thoughts and beliefs—they can induce negative changes in the body! A harmless sugar pill can induce symptoms of nausea, headaches or insomnia. The nocebo effect also explains the many adverse reactions that people experience when informed of potential side effects of a real pill. While doctors are required to inform patients of the pros and cons of a treatment, they realize that some people ruminate over the negatives. This makes them prone to fear and anxiety and consequently, the body begins to emulate the adverse symptoms the person was made aware of. The nocebo effect is again a validation of the mind-body connection.

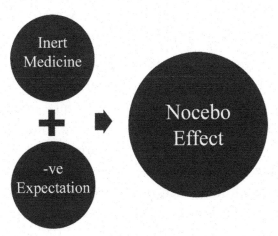

Figure 2: Negative Expectations Lead to Nocebo Effect

Most people assume that they must first become healthier, only then can they become happier. However, all these scientific studies indicate the reverse. If we become happier, we will also become healthier.

The same is true for work as well. Let us see that next.

Formula for Success: Being Happy Makes You Successful

What came first—the chicken or the egg? Does success create happiness or does happiness lead to success? Let us find out.

It has widely been accepted that working hard will make us successful, and more success will make us happier. This is the underlying formula that drives parenting and management styles. We are motivated by external goals that lie in the future.

However, the definition of success keeps getting pushed forward. Promotion at work leads to the desire for the next higher position. A pay hike inflames the craving for an even higher salary, and so on. Success, therefore, becomes a moving target. And since we imagine happiness on the other side of success, we never reach it. In fact, our physical and mental well-being get neglected when we focus on performance alone.

Modern positive psychology has consistently proven that happiness precedes success, not the other way around. In short, focusing on your happiness is a better strategy for success.

The link between well-being and life success was analysed in a massive research project spanning over 200 research studies that covered 2,75,000 people.[10] The results were revealing. Being happy unleashes mindsets that create success in every domain of life, including on the job. Happy workers are more creative and high performers. They are, hence, more likely to get promoted and get higher pay. They are also less likely to take sick leave or be prone to burnout. And it begins early on in life—people who are happy in youth tend to earn higher levels of income than their not-so-happy counterparts. Take inspiration from Michael Jordan, the 'god of basketball'.

Michael Jordan was born in a poor family living in Brooklyn, New York. When he was twelve, his father gave him an old T-shirt worth $1 and asked him to sell it for $2. While Michael could have easily dismissed the idea, he happily took up the challenge and thought of ways to do it. He tidied up the T-shirt, ironed it, and successfully sold it for $2.

---

[10] WebMD Editorial Contributors, 'Happiness Comes First, Success Follows', WebMD, 19 December 2005, https://www.webmd.com/balance/news/20051219/happiness-comes-first-success-follows.

His father again gave him a similar T-shirt worth $1 and asked him to sell it for $20. Michael was a 'go-getter'; he immediately started thinking of how to accomplish this. With the help of his friends and his creative mind, he put a Mickey Mouse sticker on the T-shirt and sold it for $20!

His dad next challenged him to sell the same T-shirt for $200. Quite the test! Again, he came up with a creative idea. Hollywood actress Farrah Fawcett had come to a nearby town for a movie shoot. He waded through the crowd to reach her and convinced her to autograph the T-shirt.

Michael then went to the market and announced that a T-shirt autographed by the famous Farrah Fawcett was on auction with a starting bid of $200. Lo and behold, it turned into a bidding rally. He finally grossed $2000 for the T-shirt.

What made Michael Jordan successful then and into his basketball career was his high-spirited personality. Right thinking, a positive mindset and the will to succeed opened the doors to success.

Advantages of happiness are not limited to individual success because happiness is contagious. One deeply optimistic team member is enough to spark an insurgence of positive emotions in the entire team. Such 'positively inspired' teams develop rapport, increase productivity and are more successful. That is why CEOs with high positive expressions are more likely to have happy employees geared for high performance. The same is also seen in team play, where one happy member uplifts the entire team.

Positivity is, therefore, a compelling factor for success. So, my advice would be to not wait for success and then become happy, but rather to be happy for achieving success.

At every moment, we have the choice to be happy or sad, and the more we choose joy, the more positive we become. The reverse also holds true—repeated thoughts of despair give us a negative filter through which we view the world. Consequently, we begin seeing pessimism and failure everywhere. Hence, the mind can either uplift our life or worsen it. The Bhagavad Gita states:

uddhared ātmanātmānaṁ nātmānam avasādayet
ātmaiva hyātmano bandhur ātmaiva ripur ātmanaḥ (6.5)

'Elevate yourself through the power of your mind, and not degrade yourself, for the mind can be the best friend and also the worst enemy of the self.'

In this chapter, we have seen the tremendous benefits of happiness. To reap them, we will need to master the art and science of happiness across all domains of life. In the forthcoming chapters, we will learn about happiness in relationships, happiness in the face of adversity, happiness at the workplace, happiness from a higher purpose, and finally, happiness from God.

The next chapter is dedicated to one of the most transformative mind management tools, called 'positive reframing'. So, let's learn about it next.

Summary

- Feeling happy has many tangible benefits and is intricately linked to the quality of our life.

- Feeling joyful makes us healthier. It boosts our immune system. A negative mood makes us prone to a variety of ailments. Anxiety puts extra strain on the heart whereas a blissful mood leads to a healthier heart. Being optimistic and harbouring a positive mindset increases vitality and lifespan.

- Happy people change their perception of stress and view difficulties as opportunities for growth.

- Happy people gravitate towards a beneficial lifestyle—regular exercise, healthy diet and better sleep.

- The placebo effect is an example of how positive beliefs can heal the body. Similarly, the nocebo effect highlights how negative thoughts and beliefs can induce negative changes in the body.

- Happiness precedes success, not the other way around. Happy workers are more creative, high performers and likely to draw higher pay.

- To reap the tremendous benefits of harbouring a positive mindset, we must train our mind to retain our happiness in every circumstance.

3

Positive Reframing

Happiness does not neatly fall into our laps. Just as physical fitness needs effort, the mind too requires training. The untrained mind is habituated to taking the path of least resistance. It easily turns pain into thoughts of suffering. People readily become dismal in the face of problems. To counter it, the art of optimism needs to be learnt and made a natural state of mind.

Positive reframing helps us do just that. It is a potent technique for changing our perspective from the deficiencies to the manifold blessings in life. It helps us see the silver lining in the worst of situations. In essence, it enables us to remain spirited through the vicissitudes of life. As you go through this chapter, you will experience that transformation for yourself. Let us get started.

Negativity Bias of Our Mind

Have you ever had a piece of fibre stuck between your teeth? A corn remnant or mango fibre—it is so annoying. Notice how your tongue repeatedly visits it and attempts to dislodge it. Amazingly, the tongue is not bothered with the twenty-seven crevices that are clean. It continually gravitates towards the one that is problematic.

Liken this to problems that come our way. Only one area in our life may be troubled, while twenty may be going well. Yet, our mind insists on revisiting that one problem area and brooding over it ceaselessly. This is because of the 'negativity bias' of our mind.

'Negativity bias' is a cognitive distortion that causes adverse events to impact our brain more deeply than positive ones. Not only do they register more quickly, but they also linger longer in our mind. That is why past hurts continue to haunt us. You remember the one critical feedback your boss gave and forget the ten good ones. Your mind keeps revisiting the single mistake you made, while ignoring the many good things you did.

Why do negative events affect us so deeply? Because the physiology of our brain is hardwired to look for adversity. In fact, the physiology of all creatures is hardwired to watch out for problems. This negativity bias of the brain enhances their chances for survival.

Let us see how this works in the case of a fish. In its environment are positive stimuli—the food it can consume. There are also negative stimuli—predators that can attack it. If the fish fails to notice opportunities for food, it is not life-threatening; more opportunities will come along. But if the fish fails to notice a predator, it becomes a fatal mistake, and the game of life is over. In this way, the negativity bias in the physiology of the fish helps to keep it safe.

Likewise, our human brain is also neurologically hardwired to watch out for negativity. Except that the adversities we face are usually not life-threatening. They are simply emotional discomforts or self-esteem issues, which are best ignored and forgotten. But when the mind insists on musing over them, it begins to wallow in negative emotions. These then become a bigger problem than the circumstance itself. For example:

- *You have a great job, but your attention repeatedly goes to the nagging colleague.*

- *Your child comes home with her report card. You ignore her four good grades, while feeling terrible about her one bad grade.*

- *Your spouse has numerous virtues, which you take for granted. Instead, you become obsessed with her one wrongdoing.*

The media is excellent at leveraging the negativity bias of individuals. It revels in creating impressions of shocking calamities and tragic happenings. Studies reveal that the more you watch television, the more likely you are to overestimate the prevalence of crime and catastrophes.[1]

Factually, in a world of eight billion people, there will always be something blowing up and someone at gunpoint. However, the probability of an individual encountering violence and crime still remains low. Further, only a very small percentage of crimes involve sex or violence. But the media's selective portrayal amplifies our perception of them manifold.

Since people prefer hearing the worst, the media has no reason to deviate from its ways. It persists in delivering bad news to get people's attention. In essence, it continues to benefit from our negativity bias.

This proclivity towards negativity acquires serious dimensions due to another brain feature, called 'neuroplasticity'. When a thought pattern is repeated again and again, the neurons get wired to revisit the same emotion more easily in future. Let us see how this happens.

---

[1] Cynthia Vinney, 'What Is Cultivation Theory in Media Psychology?', Verywell Mind, 18 January 2022, https://www.verywellmind.com/cultivation-theory-5214376.

The Tetris Effect

Tetris is a simple video game from the 1980s. It involves players stacking falling geometrical shapes neatly into a horizontal row. These shapes are in different sizes and fall from the top of the screen. Players can rotate them until they hit the bottom. The idea is to form as many unbroken horizontal rows as possible.

It seems to be a simple game but is highly addictive. Faiz Chopdat, a twenty-three-year-old Britisher, was jailed for four months after refusing to turn off his mobile on a flight because he could not stop playing Tetris.[2] That is how attention-grabbing it is!

Harvard psychiatrists studied this effect through an experiment.[3] They paid students to play Tetris for eight hours a day, three days in a row. It was any student's dream engagement—getting rewarded for playing video games. Unfortunately, they had not anticipated the colossal after-effects.

Sixty per cent of the participants saw visions of floating shapes in their dreams. Many saw the Tetris shapes in their waking state as well. They would notice cereal boxes fitting together nicely in a line in

---

[2] Shawn Achor, *The Happiness Advantage*, Virgin Books, 2011, Kindle e-book.

[3] 'The Tetris Effect: How Everything You Do Shapes Your Reality', Constant Renewal, 10 August 2022, https://constantrenewal.com/tetris-effect.

grocery aisles. They would find themselves wondering how buildings along the street could be flipped so they would form an unbroken row. They would even catch themselves calculating how to rotate bricks above to fit bricks below on a wall.

What was happening here? The brain had formed neural pathways that were primed to imagine patterns everywhere. It was a 'cognitive distortion'. This is similar to what happens if you focus on a candle flame for two minutes, and then close your eyes—you will continue to experience the flame in your mind for a while.

The Tetris Effect is not limited to gamers alone. It affects us all and bleeds into every aspect of our lives. Our brains easily get stuck in patterns of good and bad. This is because our brain is highly adaptive. Whenever we repeat thoughts in our mind, these patterns become stronger. Soon, they become part of our mindset and personality.

To illustrate this point, let me share a very interesting example of the Tetris Effect.

Shawn Achor, positive psychology researcher from Harvard, was called by KPMG, one of the biggest tax accounting firms, to help their managers feel happier.[4] KPMG had been puzzled as to why their accountants

---

[4] Shawn Achor, *The Happiness Advantage*, Virgin Books, 2011, Kindle e-book.

were so unhappy, despite being highly qualified and drawing good salaries. Achor observed that the employees were basically good people, but they had gotten caught in the Tetris Effect.

These accountants' job assignment required scanning for mistakes in account statements for more than eight hours a day. Slowly, their brains had gotten primed to look for errors, making them incredible at their jobs. The downside, unfortunately, was that they had also become experts at seeing shortcomings in their relationships and social settings.

For example, they would easily point out the weaknesses of their co-workers in performance reviews but miss out their strengths. They would see the only C grade on their child's report card, and not the A or B. They could effortlessly notice food prepared incorrectly by their spouse, but not the dainties. And a very surprising confession by one of the accountants revealed he had emailed his wife an Excel sheet with her mistakes, in an attempt to rectify her faults. She was soon to be his ex-wife!

In short, the accountants had gotten stuck in a negative Tetris Effect that had spilled over from the workplace and into their personal lives.

The same phenomenon is observed amongst lawyers as well. You will be intrigued to know that lawyers are 360 per cent more likely to suffer from depression than the general populace.[5] Why so? After all, lawyers are highly educated, they earn more than average salaries and have an engaging career.

The seed for their negative mindset gets sown in law school itself. As students, they are trained in critical thinking—to look for defects and to reject rather than to accept. This tendency to scan for negatives trickles into their lives, disrupting it. Many lawyers admit to grilling their children for the smallest mistakes. Others sheepishly confess to quantifying the time spent with their spouse in terms of the fees they charge clients per hour. It sounds terrible! But just like the accountants earlier, these lawyers too get stuck in a pattern.

Though these examples show the negative side of the Tetris Effect, the same phenomenon can be channelized in the positive direction as well. We can train our brain to see goodness and notice the abundant opportunities that exist in the same situation. We simply have to start scanning for good, hearing good things and thinking good thoughts—again and again. Positivity will then get hardwired in our brain's physiology.

Selective Perception—We See What We Want To

Innumerable stimuli impinge upon us from the outer world at every moment. We can pay attention to only

---

[5] Shawn Achor, *The Happiness Advantage*, Virgin Books, 2011, Kindle e-book.

a few of them. Based on what we choose to observe, we develop different perspectives. Selective perception explains why everyone see things differently.

For example, a food commercial will immediately grab the attention of a hungry person because it is in line with their goal of obtaining food. But it may not even register with someone shopping for a car. Similarly, a feeble cry of a baby will wake up the mother from deep sleep. The same cry would hardly be noticeable to others.

While selective perception works in our favour by keeping our attention on important matters, it can harm us too. When we are biased, consciously or unconsciously, it skews our worldview. It is easy to fall into the trap of judging people, playing favourites and becoming self-righteous. Biases negatively distort our perception of reality.

Hence, another name for selective perception is selective distortion. We filter out important information to conveniently focus our attention where we wish to. This was illustrated through one of the best-known experiments in psychology, 'The Invisible Gorilla Test'. This was a study conducted by Daniel Simons and Christopher Chabris at Harvard University in 1999.[6] It was designed to test people's awareness.

---

[6] Christopher Chabris and Daniel Simons, 'The Invisible Gorilla', The Invisible Gorilla, 10 August 2022, http://www.theinvisiblegorilla.com/gorilla_experiment.html.

Participants were asked to watch a video of two basketball teams passing a ball around. One team was dressed in black shirts and the other in white. The idea was to count the number of times the ball was passed between players wearing white shirts. At some point in the video, a woman wearing a gorilla suit walks into the middle of the scene. She faces the camera, thumps her chest and leaves. She spends roughly nine seconds on the screen.

The volunteers were asked to write down the number of passes they counted. They were further interrogated as to whether they had noticed anything unusual in the video. When confronted about the gorilla that appeared in the video, half of those watching had missed it! They sheepishly became aware of it upon re-watching the scene.

The test revealed that people can be blind to something absurdly obvious just because they are focused elsewhere. This is called 'inattentional blindness'. It explains why, when you are dying to buy the latest iPhone, you tend to notice more ads for it. The iPhone suddenly appears on Facebook or in others' hands. It is not that everyone has now switched to iPhones or that Apple has suddenly released more commercials. The advertisements were always there, and the product too has always been around. But since you had no prior need of the iPhone, it was not in your perception.

Therefore, when besieged by gloomy thoughts, do not assume it is the only perspective possible. Explore other ways of seeing and understanding the incident.

Choose to Look at Events Differently

You can see the same situation in different ways. Imagine a hot and sunny day. One person notices the beautiful sunshine, while the other observes scorching heat. Similarly, one classifies a colleague's behaviour as arrogance, while the other sees it as confidence. These are various realities in a single situation. Hence, the proverbial saying: 'Two sides of the same coin.'

A nurse at an army hospital once related to me her experience with two Indian soldiers who had been wounded in anti-terrorist operations in Kashmir. Both had unfortunately lost one leg in a grenade explosion. They had been operated upon and received an artificial limb. With it, they were learning to walk but needed a crutch for support.

The first soldier was full of complaints. He was protesting the unfair hand of God. He was cursing the terrorists and even blaming his commander for putting him on the front line.

The second soldier was brimming with gratitude. He realized he could have lost his life in the grenade explosion but was still alive to tell the tale. He saw it as God's blessing that he could sit in a wheelchair, feel the flowers much closer to him and look his little kids in the eyes!

The contrasting perspectives explained the two soldiers' experience of misery or lack of it. One saw himself as a victim, while in the same situation, the other was thrilled to see himself as a lucky survivor.

Misery is the consequence of viewing life through the lens of negativity and discontentment. In contrast, positive reframing is the art of finding the silver lining in any situation. And then focusing upon it.

So, the next time you feel anxious or depressed, simply change your viewpoint, and the door to happiness will magically open up. It does not require a key. Here is my favourite example of positive reframing.

One lady was known as the 'unhappy' lady. Nobody had ever seen her rejoicing. She happened to visit me, and I inquired about her problem.

The unhappy lady said, 'Swamiji, I have two daughters—one married a brick maker and the other wed an umbrella seller. My problem is that whenever there is rain, the first daughter complains that it will affect their brick production. And whenever there is sunshine, the second daughter complains that her umbrella sales will be affected.'

The unhappy lady continued, 'On rainy days, I think of my brick-making daughter and feel unhappy. And on sunny days, I think of my umbrella-selling daughter and feel unhappy. So, I'm always unhappy!'

I suggested a simple tweak in her thinking, 'Now do the reverse. When there is sunshine, think of your brick-making daughter's joy. On rainy days, think of how well your umbrella-selling daughter will be doing!'

With this little change, she found she could always be happy. Soon, people realized it and gave her the appellation, 'the happy lady'.

What transformed this lady from misery to joy? It was not the circumstances, just her perspective. That was enough to bring a smile on her face and contentment to her heart.

How we choose to see the world is our choice. We, by our thoughts, create the reality we live in. The Bard of Avon, Shakespeare, put it well: 'There is nothing either good or bad, but thinking makes it so.'[7]

William James expressed the same idea: 'My experience is what I agree to attend to.'[8]

---

[7] William Shakespeare, LibQuotes, https://libquotes.com/william-shakespeare/quotes/There-is-nothing-either-good-or-bad,-but-thinking-makes-it-so.

[8] William James, Quote Master, https://www.quotemaster.org/q3eee09fcf7158a57701df326cada4141.

Count Your Blessings to Reframe Negative into Positive

Much of this world and its happenings are out of our control. Anxiety attacks us because we are attached to how things 'should be' versus how 'they are'. Deficiencies that we cannot change repeatedly come to our mind. This results in discontent, causing misery.

The reverse is acceptance of things beyond our power. As the Serenity Prayer states:

O God! Grand me the serenity to bear the things I cannot change.

The strength to change the things that I can.

And the wisdom to know the difference.

These lines provide the mantra to negotiate even a tragedy with serenity. Rather than feeling miserable by focusing on what you 'lack', count your 'blessings' and fill your heart with gratitude. Learn the art from a powerful real-life story.

Anthony Ray Hinton was wrongly convicted for capital murder—a crime he did not commit.[9] *He spent thirty years on death row for no fault of his own. He had clear-cut proof of his innocence—he was working*

---

[9] 'Anthony Ray Hinton Featured on 60 Minutes', Equal Justice Initiative, 11 Jan 2016, https://eji.org/news/anthony-ray-hinton-on-60-minutes/. Accessed 6 April 2023.

in a locked factory at the time of the crime. Yet, the police blatantly informed him that he would be going to jail because he was black.

Hinton spent this time reforming himself and others. He counselled fellow inmates. The prison guards became his friends and campaigned for his exoneration. Finally, the US Supreme Court acquitted him by a unanimous ruling, and he was able to walk free.

Hinton later said in an interview: 'One does not know the value of freedom until it is taken away. People run out of the rain. I run into the rain. How can anything that falls from heaven not be precious?'

Subsequently, on 60 Minutes, *a popular American TV show, he was asked if he was angry at those who had wronged him. He said he had forgiven them all. The interviewer asked, 'But they took thirty years of your life. How can you not be angry?' Hinton responded: 'If I'm angry and unforgiving, they will have taken the rest of my life.'*

Hinton had chosen to focus on the positives in an obviously negative situation. Though his freedom was usurped, his joy and inspiration remained intact. Even more beautiful was that he saw the adversity as a grace of God. With a devotional perspective, he preferred to see his horrendous treatment as a gift he had received.

Kevin Clayson, in his bestselling book, *Flip the Gratitude Switch*, recommends we actively look for the positive in trying situations. So, the next time you face a difficult event, ask yourself, 'What is the lesson I am supposed to learn here?'

He is just echoing what Jagadguru Shree Kripaluji Maharaj taught: 'The best virtue is to force yourself to look for the positive even in the most negative circumstances.'

Sage Narad recommends the same mindset:

loka-hānau chintā na kāryā niveditātma-loka-vedatvāt
(*Narad Bhakti Darshan*, sutra 61)

'When you suffer a reversal in the world, do not lament. Choose to see benediction in the loss.'

Despite his terrible experience, Hinton did not entertain negativity in his mind. In fact, he later travelled the world to raise awareness of social injustice and help institute reform. He also published a bestselling book and was awarded an honorary doctorate by St Bonaventure University.

We too have the ability to hold on to a happy frame of mind even in the most dreadful circumstances. It is a matter of choosing to see goodness and grace. Here are some examples:

- *If you have to pay huge taxes, be thankful because it means you have a large income.*

- *If you have to clean up the mess your children create, thank God that He has blessed you with a family.*

- *If you have many chores to do at home, feel gratitude that you have a roof over your head, while so many in the world are homeless.*

- *If you have a bitter medicine to take, be thankful for it because it means you will get better.*

This kind of reframing is simple yet profoundly effective. When we decide to look at the silver lining in the cloud of adversities, we find that our worries are not as drastic as our mind makes them out to be.

Tunnel Vision Prevents Us from Practising Reframing

Positive reframing sounds simple enough in theory but can be tricky to implement. Why so? Because we are convinced our circumstances are the problem. We fail to realize the role of our mind and thoughts in creating our miserable reality. This is called 'tunnel vision'.

There was a comedy TV show in the US called The Three Stooges. *The stooges had a pet sequence they would play out. One would start screaming, 'I cannot see! I cannot see! I cannot see!'*

The second stooge would ask, 'Why not?'

The first would respond, 'Because my eyes are closed!'

The second would then bop him on the head. The first would open his eyes and exclaim, 'Thanks! I can see now.'

Similarly, our mind suffers from tunnel vision. We believe that life is oppressing us, without appreciating that we are the culprits. Our experience of happiness and distress is dependent on the manner in which we look at our circumstances. We imprison ourselves with an imperfect way of looking at things. The Vedic scriptures are thus called *Darshan Shastras*, or holy books that enable us to truly see.

From our perspective, pain is a bad thing, while pleasure is most desirable. Contrarily, the Vedas guide us to make self-growth our goal and not the maximization of pleasure. The perspective of self-improvement empowers us to see grace in both good and bad situations.

In fact, the *Darshan Shastras* go a step further and tell us the whole world is the veritable form of God. The *Īśhāvāsya Upanishad* states:

īśhā vāsyam-idaṁ sarvaṁ yat-kiñcha jagatyāṁ jagat

'All that exists in the universe is a manifestation of the Supreme Lord.' The Bhagavad Gita states:

vāsudevaḥ sarvam iti   (verse 7.19)

'The Supreme Lord is all that is.' And Sage Tulsidas states in the Ramayan:

sīyā rāmamaya saba jaga jānī,
    karauñ pranām jori juga pānī

'The whole world is full of the presence of Sita Ram. Hence, I fold my hands and offer my respects to all.'

All these scriptures reiterate that the world created by God is auspicious and divine. We must get out of our tunnel vision and adopt new ways of reasoning based on higher wisdom. The shift in perspective will release us from the shackles of despair.

Put It to Practice—How to Reframe Daily Life

When negative thoughts crop up, here are some questions to examine your thinking. Asking yourself these questions will allow you to see your personal experiences in a larger way. They will make you aware of any faulty inner beliefs you may be holding on to.

- *Is what I am thinking true? Can it be verified with evidence?*

- *Does such thinking align with my values, such as kindness, compassion, forgiveness, selflessness and empathy? Is it in accordance with the teachings of my Guru and the scriptures?*

- *Is there a better way of thinking about this? Or another way of looking at this situation?*

one. Instead, be open to other happier viewpoints. At the same time, have faith that the Universe is benevolent, and all reversals have silver linings; you just have to look hard enough to find them. Doing so opens up the doorway to discovering goodness and joy in every situation.

The next chapter delves into the good and bad kinds of happiness and shows how lasting fulfilment comes from finding a higher purpose in life.

Summary

- We all suffer from a negativity bias, which causes adverse events to impact our brain more deeply than positive ones.

- Whenever we repeat thoughts in our mind, these patterns become stronger. This is the Tetris Effect.

- Repeated negative thoughts wire us for negativity. Repeated positive thoughts wire us to scan for good, hear good and think good.

- Misery is the consequence of viewing life through the lens of negativity and discontentment. In contrast, positive reframing is the art of finding the silver lining in all situations.

- We all have the ability to respond with a happy frame of mind, even in dreadful circumstances. It is a matter of choosing to see the good and learning to be grateful.

- Positive reframing is a potent technique that changes our perspective from the deficiencies to the manifold blessings in life.

- Positive reframing is tricky to implement because we fail to realize the role of our mind in creating our miserable reality. This is called 'tunnel vision'. We must adopt new ways of reasoning based on higher wisdom.

4

Happiness from Finding a Higher Purpose in Life

Where does happiness lie and what should we do to get it? Materialists tell us to eat, drink and be merry; spiritualists suggest we seek peace within ourselves. Sages teach selfless service; lay people recommend selfish pursuits. The West emphasizes acquisition; the East teaches letting go. Which is the right path to a joyous life?

Well, it is commonly said, 'We are spiritual beings having a material experience.' Spiritual perfection will undoubtedly bestow everlasting divine happiness. However, until we reach there, we must also master the art and science of finding joy in our material activities. This requires understanding the correlation between external objects and inner bliss.

We will start with the most fundamental question related to happiness.

Can Money Buy Happiness?

An increase in wealth has many benefits. Economic progress eradicates poverty and unemployment. It improves the standard of living by helping us purchase more amenities for our comforts. So far, so good! Money and growth must make us happy then? Or is prosperity overstated? Let us find out.

Money can buy us the things of the world. Without it, we cannot meet our basic needs of food, clothing and shelter. The toys we loved as kids were purchased with money by our parents. Our first apartment, first car and first vacation were all procured through currency. Hence, from an early age, our mind learnt to associate pleasure with money. But does that mean money makes us happy? No!

World economic data reveals that the average person in the world today is 4.4 times richer than in 1950.[1] Growth and prosperity today allow us to purchase beyond mere need. We can now venture into comforts and luxuries. With the global mean household income improving, homes today are larger, gadgets abound and luxuries have become common. Despite all this, the number of people saying they are happy has reduced. Why this paradox?

---

[1] Max Roser, 'Economic Growth', OurWorldInData.org, 2013, https://ourworldindata.org/economic-growth#citation. Accessed 13 August 2022.

Numerous studies attest that money cannot buy happiness.[2] Almost all philosophical traditions also state the same. Two thousand years ago, Roman philosopher, Seneca, said: 'Money has yet to make anyone rich.' Why have philosophers taken this view? Understand it from your own experience of life.

In college, when you bought a motorcycle, it gave a kick. But its thrill soon faded, and then to get the same kick you needed a Maruti Suzuki—the basic model car. Yet, with time, its pleasure too disappeared, and then you desired a Honda. After a while, the Honda became your norm, and you sought the excitement of driving a Mercedes.

The learning is that pleasures we cherish provide a thrill for only a little while after their acquisition. Soon they become mundane as the 'high' wears off. Then, our mind looks for the next 'kick', usually at an even higher cost.

Think about it. When you were in school, a day trip would satisfy, but on entering college, you needed a vacation in Goa. And a few years into your career, the idea of a Goa holiday seemed bland. Now, for the same joy, you craved a pleasure trip to Europe.

---

[2] Michael S. James, 'Study: Money, Luxury Can't Buy Happiness', ABC News, 11 February 2001, https://abcnews.go.com/Health/story?id=116613&page=1.

However, this cycle does not satiate. The standard of living keeps increasing, but it does not directly translate to a better quality of life. We drive a Mercedes to get from point A to B, while the Maruti Suzuki could do the same. We pay through our nose to fly first class, whereas economy gets us to the same destination. We want a Rolex, while an HMT tells the same time.

In fact, by increasing our external standards, we take on more responsibilities, creating more worries. Burdens of house, job, taxes and bills consume us. We reach a fulfilment ceiling beyond which wealth and its upkeep actually work against us. The double-storeyed house and expensive car do not provide the joy that carefree walks in the park gave us as poor college students.

This explains the happiness paradox the world faces today. Though economic growth has provided greater prosperity, we are tottering under the burden of enhanced responsibilities. Externally, we put on the facade of thriving, while internally, we feel drained. Renowned psychologist, Viktor Frankl, in his book *Man's Search for Meaning*, lamented that 25 per cent of his European students and 60 per cent of his American students felt an 'inner emptiness, a void within themselves'.[3]

---

[3] Viktor Frankl, *Man's Search for Meaning: Young Adult Edition*, Boston: Beacon Press, Logotherapy in a Nutshell (Abridged), 2017, Kindle e-book.

The situation is worse today than decades ago when Frankl authored his book. While wealth has multiplied two to three times in developed nations, depression, divorce, teen suicide—all are on the rise in unprecedented numbers. Thus, money alone cannot make us happy.

Fulfilment Curve

Once you are above the poverty line, you have clothing, food and a roof over your head. Then, an extra bonus from work does not radically change your joy. At this stage, the correlation between wealth and happiness becomes smaller. Comforts such as larger homes, more cars and gadgets become the norm of life.

The happiness from money reaches a peak at one point. If you spend more than that 'sweet spot', your happiness begins to dwindle. To explain this, Joe Dominguez and Vicki Robin coined the term 'Fulfilment Curve'.[4] They divided spending into four stages: survival, comforts, luxuries and overconsumption.

Survival. These are base-level needs that must be met for subsistence. They include food, shelter, clothing and basic transportation. Spending on them is a necessary use of our money. It drastically boosts our satisfaction

---

[4] Vicki Robin and Joe Dominguez, *Your Money or Your Life*, Penguin Books, Second Revised Edition, 2018, Kindle e-book.

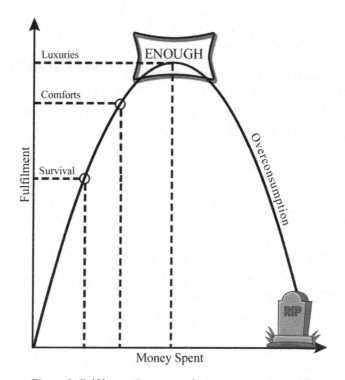

Figure 3: Fulfilment Curve correlating money spent with happiness achieved.

level. Compare it to walking into a warm home during a cold winter night. Or liken it to resting after slogging twelve hours at work.

Comforts. These are commodities that improve our standard of living. They include healthy entertainment, occasional restaurant meals and shoes for different occasions. Though not vital, they are nice to have. These increase our happiness, but the spending on these does not boost our happiness as much as it did on elemental needs. Notice how the curve is still positive but not as steep as the 'survival' phase.

Luxuries. This is the last leap of spending that improves our joy. Perhaps a sports car, an expensive dress or jewellery. These can be classified as luxuries that lie beyond mere comforts. They require higher income and push you to the pinnacle of the Fulfilment Curve.

Overconsumption. It includes high-end luxuries and indulgences. In this stage, elite consumer goods and an extravagant lifestyle overtake you. Your house fills up with 'stuff' as you find yourself at shopping malls every week. Maintenance of such a lifestyle robs you of happiness. It pushes you to work harder to keep up with your rich neighbour and sucks fulfilment out of life.

From the Fulfilment Curve, we can conclude that happiness from money peaks in the 'luxuries' phase. Your basic needs are provided for, you have decent comforts and a few luxuries. An equilibrium of spending and happiness is achieved, and hence you have 'enough'. But rarely are we satisfied with 'enough'. In fact, we do not even know what is 'enough'. So, let's attempt to learn it from the story below.

A king once organized a competition in his capital to find a wise minister. Thousands participated for the grand prize, which was to be appointed as the king's minister.

The king placed valuable items in his beautiful garden without any mention of their value. The rule was: Whoever finds the most precious item in the garden and presents it before the king will be the winner.

The competition began with great enthusiasm and fervour. Participants searched for items of value, and if they found a goodie, they brought it to the king with anticipation. But none created a big impact on him.

A little while later, a young man appeared empty-handed in front of the king. 'Did you not find anything of value in the garden?' asked the king.

The man replied, 'Your Highness, I have come with the most valuable item.'

'What is it?' questioned the king, puzzled. 'You are carrying nothing.'

The man replied with a beaming smile, 'I have come with contentment. With a discontented mindset, nothing is ever enough. But one who is contented feels no lack.'

The king was highly impressed and awarded him the prize.

That is why the Vedic scriptures call 'contentment' as the highest wisdom. Sage Bhartrihari said:

sa tu bhavati daridrī yasya tṛiṣhṇā viśhālā,
manasi cha parituṣhṭe ko 'arthavān ko daridraḥ

(*Vairagya Śhatak*)

'That person is penurious whose desires are many. One whose mind is content is never poor.'

In conclusion, we must have enough money to secure our present and future needs. But wealth cannot buy long-lasting fulfilment. In the US, top basketball and football players earn in the range of fifty million dollars every year. Yet, more than 60 per cent become impoverished within years of retirement. The same is witnessed with lottery winners, many of whom go bankrupt, face divorce, get jailed or are murdered. A sudden windfall clouds their judgement. They spend indiscriminately on fancier homes, lavish vacations and friends. Soon, they find themselves in a worse condition than before they had hit the jackpot. On the contrary, self-made millionaires are prudent with their money. They live an average lifestyle—normal cars, simple neighbourhoods and hard work. Irrespective of their income, they keep their spending in check and remain grounded.

Having said that, do note one valuable use for money that always remains—it can be used to purchase beautiful life experiences. For example, if you desire a trip to Ladakh in the Himalayas, it cannot be done without money. And such an experience is more valuable than the new car you purchase. Hence, money does contribute to experiential happiness which is far greater than possessive happiness. Let me explain that next.

Life Experiences Can Increase Our Happiness Even beyond Luxuries

Assets are not merely a net-sum of material possessions. They also include memorable experiences of the external world and the learning of new skills that add value to our life. The joyous memories they help create, the interpersonal bonds we forge through them and the satisfaction they bestow remain with us for a lifetime.

There are several reasons why experiences give more joy than possessions. Firstly, experiences are personal, and hence, a more meaningful part of one's identity. They shift our focus from 'having' to 'doing'. They leave lasting impressions and learnings. Through them, we enhance our appreciation of the world around us. Besides, we are less likely to compare them with others since they are unique to us as individuals. In contrast, possessions, such as a home or car, can easily put us in the mode of 'keeping up with the Joneses'.

Secondly, experiences often require overcoming challenges and accomplishing tasks. They broaden our perspective and provide avenues for inner growth. They come with stories that can be talked about and shared with others. These are more significant than mere objects. This multiplies their pleasure.

Thirdly, in the pursuit of experiences, social bonds are fostered. We form memories and create ties with each other that could last a lifetime. No amount of material possessions can give us the joy that comes from human interaction.

Finally, while material goods diminish in value, experiences appreciate with time, generating more happiness. For example, memories of a summer camp from your childhood may still spark happiness in you today. You are likely to have a smile on your face as you recall the beautiful sunshine, the frolic with friends or the excitement of your first campfire. On the other hand, selecting an HDTV from the dozens of choices can leave you frustrated and confused. Add to it the need for having a comparable one to your friends.

Thus, experiences are a meaningful form of assets. They provide happiness that lasts longer than mere material commodities. That said, our search for happiness is still not quenched. We must endeavour for a kind of happiness that cannot be purchased, rather, it is cultivated within ourselves. Let us then keep moving forward in our search.

Immediate Thrill vs Long-Term Fulfilment

Life puts a variety of joys on our platter, and we must choose from them. The paradox is that worthwhile pleasures lie upstream—to earn them requires effort and self-discipline. On the other hand, harmful delights are often just an arm's length away.

For example, to be a couch potato needs no effort, but to achieve good health, we must go through the drudgery of daily exercise and a healthy diet. Likewise, venting our anger on a loved one is easy. But to apologize and save a relationship—even though it hurts the ego—is difficult.

Mark Twain very aptly said: 'The only way to keep your health is to eat what you do not want, drink what you do not like, and do what you'd rather not.'

This is applicable to all facets of life. The Vedas speak of two kinds of pleasures: *śhreya* and *preya*. *Śhreya* is the kind of happiness that is bitter initially but becomes sweet later. In contrast, *preya* is that happiness which is sweet at first but turns into poison later.

For example, most students, if they have a choice, prefer watching movies to studying. However, success in school requires consistent effort. Those who pick *śhreya* deny immediate gratification and work hard to achieve their goal. While those who pick *preya* watch a Netflix movie only to fail their upcoming exam.

The end result of each choice is bluntly different. The *Kaṭhopaniṣhad* states:

anyachchhreyo 'nyadutaiva preyaste
  ubhe nānārthe puruṣhañ sinītaḥ
tayoḥ śhreya ādadānasya sādhu bhavati
  hīyate 'rthādya u preyo vṛiṇīte
śhreyaśhcha preyaśhcha manuṣhyameta-stau
  samparītya vivinakti dhīraḥ
śhreyo hi dhīro 'bhi preyaso vṛiṇīte
  preyo mando yogakṣhemād vṛiṇīte   (1.2.1–2)

'There are two paths—one is "beneficial" and the other is "pleasant". These two lead humans to very different ends. The pleasant is enjoyable in the beginning but it ends in pain. The ignorant are snared to the pleasant and perish. But the wise are not deceived by its attractions. They choose the beneficial and finally attain true happiness.'

Lasting happiness requires selecting the more difficult path—we must reject *preya* and select *śhreya*. Yet, it is in this very process that we often stumble. Let me share my own experience.

Many years ago, I was travelling in a bus in Delhi. A tramp was sitting next to me. We both got off at the same bus stop. That was when I noticed he was limping. I looked at his feet and saw he was wearing a high-heeled sandal on one foot, while the other foot was bare.

'O my dear fellow, have you lost a sandal?' I asked him.

With a smirk, the tramp replied, 'No, Babaji. I found a sandal!'

This was a classic case of self-inflicted misery. There was no compulsion to wear the sandal, simply because he had found it. By choosing to put it on, he had brought pain to himself. Similarly, we make wrong choices and subsequently suffer the consequences.

The Vedic perspective of *shreya* and *preya* finds its parallel in modern psychology. The nomenclature it uses is hedonic and eudemonic happiness. These two terms come from Greek philosophy. Let us understand them next.

Hedonia—The Happiness Trap

Psychology studies both the short- and long-term paths to happiness. The hedonistic tendency is to go for the 'feel good' activities that provide short bursts of delight. Some examples of hedonic pleasures are eating exotic foods, purchasing luxury cars and a late-night dance party.

The sense of well-being from hedonic delights is immediate, but this evaporates later. In fact, it inflames your desires for more indulgence. Think of the times you pampered yourself with unhealthy sweets, bought expensive fashionable clothes or took an extravagant vacation—these made you happy but only temporarily. They left you hankering for more such experiences.

As a result, after years of chasing hedonic pleasures, you find yourself no better off than before. This phenomenon is called the 'hedonic treadmill', akin to running on a treadmill while still remaining in the same place. It can also be compared to a mouse on the inner rim of a wheel—it runs like crazy, yet stays put at the same place. Likewise, hedonic pleasures bind us in desires for enjoyment and create a yearning for more, without increasing our overall happiness.

That is how kids get hooked to video games or adults to alcohol. One innocuous social drink with friends gives a thrill. They look forward to experiencing that repeatedly. And before they realize it, they are caught in the habit of drinking daily. Soon the habit grips them so strongly that they find it almost impossible to release themselves from its clutches.

Additionally, many hedonic activities result in an unhealthy lifestyle if we are not careful in limiting them. You start treating yourself to chocolate cake after dinner every day. A month later, you realize you have gained five pounds! A simple pleasure has now turned problematic.

There is yet another problem. Hedonists seek happiness by avoiding pain. If work is difficult, they prefer to escape it, though it may be of high value. Suppose, for example, a pleasure-seeker gets into a relationship with great excitement. Then the realization dawns that maintaining it will require bearing pain. So, the pleasure-seeker speedily moves on to the next relationship. In this way, momentary gratification is what counts for the hedonist personality type, who prefers the pleasurable over the beneficial.

From the above analysis, it is aptly clear that hedonism will not quench our thirst for lasting happiness. Shree Krishna validates the same in the Bhagavad Gita:

ā-brahma-bhuvanāl lokāḥ punar āvartino 'rjuna
mām upetya tu kaunteya punar janma na vidyate

(verse 8.16)

The wisdom from this verse is that if we seek happiness in external objects, we will continue rotating in the cycle of samsara. However, if we turn our mind away from sensual pleasures, we will gradually develop an elevated state of consciousness, and there will be no further rebirth.

This will not happen on its own; it will require effort. The next half of the chapter explains the progression towards it.

Eudaimonia—Happiness That Builds Character

Etymologically, 'eudaimonia' comprises the prefix *eu*, meaning 'good', and *daimon*, meaning 'spirit or true self'. It is a state of positive well-being aligned with your true self. Hence, eudaimonia refers to well-being associated with pursuing meaningful goals that provide a sense of fulfilment. These include personal growth, striving for excellence and a higher purpose in life. They result in lasting bliss. They also help unleash the infinite potential of your soul.

Notice how long-term fulfilment—eudemonic joy—involves effort and patience, while hedonic pleasure is easy entertainment. Hence, hedonia and eudaimonia are stark opposites. One ignites craving, while the other brings contentment. One brings comfort, while the other challenges and rewards with satisfaction. One is momentary, while the other is evolutionary.

Here are some examples of eudemonic pursuits:

- *Studying hard for exams to secure a bright career.*

- *Saving money by giving up immediate pleasures for a comfortable retirement.*

- *Exercising daily to develop good health.*

- *Forgoing junk food to enhance physical fitness.*

- *Displaying tolerance and acceptance in relationships to ensure harmony.*

- *Sacrificing time, effort and money to volunteer for a noble cause.*

- *Relinquishing sleep to wake up early for spiritual practice.*

- *Using your talents in the service of others.*

- *Stepping outside your comfort zone and taking on a challenging project.*

- *Focusing on becoming the best version of yourself, without comparing with others.*

In each of these activities, we forgo present pleasure for greater future gain. The beneficial results come later, while the toil and hard work come now. Eudemonic well-being does not ensure a pain-free existence, rather, it engenders self-improvement. This gives us a sense of accomplishment that lasts well beyond the process.

Eudemonic activities build character. They inspire us to live virtuously and demand commitment to excellence. The growth stays with us forever, helping us face life with more confidence and hope.

An important aspect of eudaimonia is finding a higher purpose and aligning your life with it.

Happiness from a Sense of Purpose

It is commonly said that if you have not found a cause you are willing to die for, your life is not worth living. But the reverse is also true; a strong sense of purpose enables us to easily navigate adversities.

A retired chief engineer of Odisha, an elderly gentleman, was suffering from depression and came to me for help. His wife, whom he loved beyond anything in the world, had died, leaving a terrible void in his life. They had fallen in love fifty-five years ago and had lived for fifty years as husband and wife. They had been each other's support in the inevitable challenges that had come their way. They had raised three children, who were now well-settled. But recently, the harsh hand of death had snatched the gentleman's wife away from him, and he was immersed in immeasurable grief.

Since he was seeking help, I pondered on what to say to him. If I said, 'It was your destiny', he would have continued to feel miserable on having such a bad destiny.

If I suggested, 'It was the will of God', he would have been resentful of God.

Instead, I inquired, 'Did your wife love you very much?'

His eyes lit up as he responded, 'Swamiji, immeasurably!'

'Suppose you had left the world before her,' I asked. 'How would she have borne that grief?'

'Swamiji, she would have been shattered,' he said. 'There would be no way she could have tolerated that misery.'

I then explained, 'You know, by outliving your wife you have saved her from immense pain.'

All of a sudden, a light went on in his head. He realized a higher purpose was being served by his suffering. He had saved his wife from misery. For the first time in many months, he smiled and left.

There was no way for me to bring back his wife for him. But by helping him find meaning in suffering, I enabled him to cope with it.

The uncommonly known secret is that humans willingly bear the severest hardships when they find it is aligned with a purpose they firmly believe in. For example, when Olympic athletes prepare, they exert themselves until every muscle in their body is aching. But that pain does not make them sad. It exhilarates them with the euphoric fulfilment of exerting themselves to the utmost for a higher objective they are convinced is valuable.

If you have a strong enough why, you willingly bear any hardship. That is why, Friedrich Nietzsche, the German philosopher, said: 'He who has a "why" to live for can bear almost any "how".'[5]

---

[5] If We Have Our Own 'Why' of Life, We Shall Get Along With Almost Any 'How', The Quote Investigator, https://quoteinvestigator. com/2019/10/09/why. Accessed 6 April 2023.

On the other hand, there are people who live in luxury—a life devoid of discomfort—and yet they are depressed. These are the people who have enough to live by but nothing to live for. Their unhappiness proves the adage that 'man does not live by bread alone'.

Finding Your Purpose in Life

How do we know that we have found our purpose? If we wake up in the morning with gratitude and look forward to a day of meaningful toil, enthusiastic to do our best, it indicates we have found a purpose for our life. On the other hand, if our first act upon waking in the morning is searching for entertainment on social media, it means we are still purposeless.

Everyone's life purpose is different. For some, it comes about through their profession, while others find it in a social cause. Yet others discover it in creative pursuits. For some, a spiritual belief leads to it. Many times, people find deeper meaning from suffering. Pain can lead to new insights, which helps us to discover a deeper meaning of life.

Let me share an inspiring example of someone who was thrown into adversity but found meaning in helping others.

Sindhutai Sapkal was born in the district of Wardha, an arid region of Maharashtra. When she was six years old, she used to take her family's buffaloes for grazing. After the buffaloes were immersed in the lake, Sindhu would go to school. There she was beaten by her teachers for coming late. After school, she would return to the buffaloes, and the neighbouring farmers would beat her because her buffaloes had strayed into their fields.

When she was merely twelve, her poor parents married her off to someone more than double her age. From her husband, she had three children. By the time she was expecting a fourth child, she had become an activist. Sindhu saw the local mafia exploit women for gathering cow dung. She reported the matter to the district collector. This annoyed the mafia. The head of their gang plotted against Sindhu. He went and told her husband that Sindhu was having a secret affair with him, and the child in her womb was his, not her husband's.

The gullible husband believed him and became enraged. He kicked Sindhu in the stomach multiple times, until she fainted. Assuming her to be dead, he threw her in the cowshed, thinking that the cows would trample her, and no one would know the real cause of her death. However, as luck would have it, a cow stood over her in protection. At night, she delivered her fourth child. In the absence of any maternity facilities or midwife, she cut the umbilical cord with a stone.

Sindhu took her newborn and walked to her parents'
home. They refused to take her in. Now, she had nowhere
to go. To avoid abuse, she began living in a nearby
cremation ground. There would be occasions when she
would gather raw grain fallen in the marketplace and
cook it on the funeral pyres burning in the cremation
ground. Many a time she thought of committing suicide
and putting an end to her disgusting life.

On one such occasion, she lay down on the railway
track with her baby. Right then, she heard the wailing
of an old and hungry man. She got up to provide him
solace and food. This gave her a sense of fulfilment.
It made her think, 'Can I find purpose in my life by
serving others?' But she thought again, 'When I do not
have anything myself, what can I give to anyone else?'

At that time, Sindhu's attention went to the branch
of the tree under which she was sitting. It was partially
broken and was dangling; yet it was providing her with
shade from the scorching sun. Sindhu got her answer
and decided, 'If this pitiable branch can serve me, I can
also do some good for others.'

She took three abandoned children at the railway
station under her care. She would beg for them and
feed them. Soon the number of children grew to fifteen.
This attracted the attention of well-minded people,
who began assisting her. They built her a shelter, and
she became known as 'Mother of the Orphans'. In

order to ensure no bias, she gave her own child away to an orphanage.

With time, Sindhu raised more and more children. Many of them became graduates, postgraduates and even PhDs. Her own children got to know of her work and came to help her. Sindhu said the crowning moment was when a wretched old man came to her for shelter. On closer observation, she realized it was her husband. She took him in, not as a spouse, but as a child. She would joke, 'He is my naughtiest child.'

Sindhutai Sapkal was a blazing example of someone who overcame adversity to find deeper meaning in her life. The Mother of the Orphans received about 350 international awards for her work, including the Padma Shri from the Government of India. In March 2021, JKYog conferred upon her the Lifetime Achievement Award for Women. During her acceptance speech, the inner joy reflecting on her face was unforgettable.

The higher purpose you determine for yourself should be so inspiring that pursuing it brings out your best qualities. It should exemplify who you are and what you believe in. It can even change as you go through life.

Pointers to your purpose can come by pondering over the following questions:

- *Why am I here?*
- *What is the goal of human life?*

- *How can I contribute my talents to society and make a difference?*

- *What will give me inner happiness and peace?*

Let the answers to these questions serve as a compass to lead you in the direction of growth and fulfilment. In the next chapter, we will discuss how to face adversity and remain happy in the face of it.

Summary

- On our journey to spiritual perfection, we must also learn the art of finding joy in our material activities.

- Money cannot buy lasting happiness. People are richer today than ever before, yet the number of people saying they are happy has reduced.

- Life experiences give more happiness than possessions. Experiences are meaningful, form beautiful memories and create lasting social ties.

- The Vedas speak of two kinds of pleasures: *shreya* and *preya*. *Shreya* is like poison at first but turns into nectar later. *Preya* is like nectar in the beginning but later becomes like poison.

- The same perspective is paralleled in modern psychology's classification of happiness—hedonia and eudaimonia. The sense of well-being from hedonic delights is immediate but evaporates later.

- In contrast, eudaimonia refers to well-being associated with pursuing meaningful goals that make your life purposeful and provide a sense of fulfilment.

- Having a sense of purpose in life provides sustained gratification. A strong sense of purpose enables us to easily navigate adversities.

- The higher purpose you determine for yourself should be so inspiring that pursuing it brings out your best.

5

Happiness in the Face of Adversity

In Indian families, with the arrival of a newborn, parents often call in the family astrologer to predict the baby's destiny. The *jyotashi* prepares the *janama kundali* (birth chart). Suppose, the astrologer reads from the chart:

> Until the age of nine, the baby will suffer from a lot of health issues. At eighteen, he will crack the IIT entrance examination. At twenty, he will be injured in a major car accident. At twenty-four, your child will become an entrepreneur, launching his own business. At thirty, he will marry outside his religion, causing you great distress. But three years later, he will become the chief technology officer of a multinational corporation. Severe marital issues to the extent of divorce are looming around the age of thirty-five.

Personally, I am a firm believer in the power of self-effort and do not recommend getting predictions or solutions from astrologers. However, suppose, to undo your child's bad fate, the family astrologer recommends you meet a specific baba (renunciate) with occult powers. The baba gives you a magical pen that allows you to edit your child's destiny. What would you do? Like most parents, you would strike off all the traumas and heave a sigh of relief.

While this act would be with the good intention to protect your child, it could actually harm the little life in blossoming to its best. How? A larva cut open from a cocoon fails to transform into a butterfly. It needs the struggle of escaping from the cocoon to develop its wings. Similarly, complete erasure of hardships from your child's future would leave him or her emotionally and spiritually immature.

The truth is that problems and adverse circumstances are inevitable. Ill health, financial loss, betrayal and natural calamities are all built into the canvas of life. Though we prefer they did not exist, difficult situations do serve a purpose. It is for us to find meaning in unpleasantness and learn to be happy amidst adversity.

The first few sections of this chapter explain the benefits of adverse situations. We will then delve into inner growth as a result of suffering, with spiritual insights.

Failure Is Just One Node in the Journey of Life

A failure is just one amongst the many million data points that define your personality. In the bigger picture, who you are is defined by the sum total of all those data points, and not any one single event. Realizing that failure is normal helps us accept it in our daily life. With acceptance, the negative emotions associated with failure begin to fade.

Here is my favourite example of someone who:

- *Failed in business and went bankrupt at the age of twenty-three.*

- *Failed again in business at the age of twenty-four.*

- *Lost the love of his life to death at the age of twenty-six.*

- *Had a nervous breakdown at the age of twenty-seven.*

- *Remarried but lost two children at the age of thirty-three.*

- *Lost a congressional race at the age of thirty-four.*

- *Lost a congressional race again at the age of thirty-six.*

- *Lost a senatorial race at the age of forty-five.*

- *Failed in an effort to become vice president at the age of forty-seven.*

- *Lost a senatorial race at the age of forty-seven.*

Despite these failures, he never quit and was finally elected as the sixteenth President of the United States at the age of fifty-two!

You can likely guess who he was. Abraham Lincoln, the most inspiring President of America. He was born in penury and yet created history. He persevered despite the many failures he endured. His motto was simple: 'When I do good, I feel good. When I do bad, I feel bad. That is my religion.'

Unbeknownst to him, Lincoln was living the philosophy of the Bhagavad Gita:

kāyena manasā buddhyā kevalair indriyair api
yoginaḥ karma kurvanti saṅgaṁ tyaktvātma-śhuddhaye

(verse 5.11)

'The yogis, while giving up attachment, perform actions with their body, senses, mind and intellect only for the purpose of self-purification.'

If you examine the lives of other great leaders, you will find their journey also strewn with a multitude of failures. Yet they did not collapse under pressure. They had learnt the art of overcoming all obstacles. Ryan Holiday, in his bestselling book, *The Obstacle Is the Way*, shares examples from the lives of many such luminaries who exhibited this trait. He says, 'Great individuals . . . find a way to transform weakness into strength. It's a rather amazing and even touching feat.

They took what should have held them back and used it to move forward.'

Benjamin Franklin stated: 'Things which hurt, instruct.'

Therefore, **when you hit upon what may seem like a failure, realize that it is not the end of life. In fact, with deeper insight, it can be the raw material for a successful journey ahead.** Let us learn how.

How Physical Pain Can Serve a Higher Purpose

Imagine a life without pain. No throbbing headaches; no aching joints; no backaches. Does it sound like a big relief? Think again. Physical pain is not a nuisance; it serves a purpose. It is a perception of the nervous system. It informs you of what is happening in your own body.

For athletes, physical pain is part of their daily routine. They push through it, to rise up in their game. In monkhood too, enduring physical pain is considered critical to spiritual growth. But how can physical pain be beneficial? This counter-intuitive truth was revealed in a study of leprosy patients.

Dr Brand was a world-renowned surgeon. He had spent his childhood years in India where leprosy piqued his curiosity, and he was determined to help affected patients. Dr Brand's studies led him to the startling conclusion that the wasting away of the limbs was not because of the leprosy bacterium, as had earlier been thought. Rather, it happened because the bacteria extinguished the sensation of pain in the body. This was the most destructive aspect of the disease since patients ended up injuring themselves due to their insensitivity. Without pain, patients would walk with torn skin or stick their hands in a fire to retrieve something.[1]

The leprosy studies revealed that pain is not an enemy, as is universally considered. It is, in fact, a remarkable and sophisticated biological system that warns us of injury to the body and thus protects us from further damage.

If we keep this understanding, we will not be disturbed when pain strikes. This does not imply that we invite pain, rather, we accept it graciously when it comes. Such a positive mindset reduces suffering from pain perception.

This is not to deny the need for medical treatment of physical injury. The point is to keep a healthy attitude towards pain and its discomfort. View it not as a punishment but as an opportunity for improvement. Let us see next how it helps us in the professional field.

---

[1] International Leprosy Association, 'Dr Paul Wilson Brand', International Leprosy Association—History of Leprosy, https://leprosyhistory.org/database/person31. Accessed 30 September 2022.

Adversity Opens Inconceivable Doors to Professional Success

We all love and celebrate success. On the flip side, its opposite, a loss, is something we dread. But challenges and setbacks are not necessarily bad. They all have a silver lining, if we choose to see it. Enduring them propels our flight to the highest peaks and holds the key to success, as we shall soon see.

At the Kellogg School of Management, researchers utilized advanced analytics to assess the relationship between early professional failure and later-life success.[2] As compared to the popular norm, they found that failure early in one's career leads to greater success in the long term for those who retain a positive attitude and keep trying.

On the other hand, absence of hardships retards growth. Not only is it unrealistic but also not necessarily healthy. The German philosopher, Friedrich Nietzsche, eloquently stated: 'What does not kill me, makes me stronger.'[3]

---

[2] 'Science Demonstrates That What Doesn't Kill You Makes You Stronger, *ScienceDaily*, 1 October 2019, https://www.sciencedaily.com/releases/2019/10/191001084008.htm. Accessed 25 February 2022.

[3] Friedrich Nietzsche, LibQuotes, https://libquotes.com/friedrich-nietzsche/quote/lbw0l9e.

An inspirational role model of an ordinary person who evolved through life's challenges is the most popular President of India since its independence, Dr A.P.J. Abdul Kalam.

Abdul Kalam had humble beginnings as a ferryman's youngest child, in South India's small pilgrimage town of Rameswaram. Despite his family's penury, his dedication to academics landed him a scholarship to the Madras Institute of Technology. After completing a degree in aeronautical engineering, he was interviewed by the Indian Air Force but did not qualify to join. His cherished dream of becoming a fighter pilot was shattered. He then joined the Ministry of Defence, in its newly formed wing, Defence Research and Development Organisation (DRDO).

From there, Dr Kalam was sent on deputation to the Indian Space Research Organisation (ISRO), when it was just in its nascent stage. With limited resources, in 1963 he helped launch India's first sounding rocket. From 1969, he worked incessantly, as the director of ISRO, on a Satellite Launch Vehicle (SLV), without much funding from the government. Despite so much hard work, the first SLV launch in 1979 was a failure. Persistent efforts led to grand success in the subsequent year, 1980.

From 1982 to 1985, Dr Kalam and his team succeeded in making many kinds of guided missiles. However, their endeavours to make Agni, a long-range missile, failed multiple times and created a lot of embarrassment in the media. Dr Kalam persevered until Agni was a success, which put India amongst the elite group of six nations with long-range missile technology. He then became known as the 'Missile Man of India'.

In 1992, Dr Kalam pioneered Operation Shakti for developing indigenous nuclear technology. In 1998, Dr Kalam and his team succeeded in detonating five nuclear devices of successively higher intensities, announcing the nuclear strength of India to the world, for protecting its sacred territories.

In 2014, the groundwork laid by him led to India's Mangalyan project, the cheapest spacecraft to reach Mars, that too on the first attempt. It was followed by the launch of 104 satellites through a single rocket in 2017. This was the world's most affordable space programme!

Dr Kalam faced immense challenges along the way. However, he never used these as excuses for failure. His philosophy was simple—when problems besiege one, refuse to be defeated and persist in the face of them. His life was a blazing example of perseverance in the midst of difficulties.

Let us next see how tragedy can benefit our relationships.

Silver Lining in the Loss of a Loved One

Few things can compare to the grief upon the loss of a loved one. While it can feel overwhelming, it too has its silver lining and teachings. It can help strengthen existing relationships. It can also help manifest positive qualities that were dormant and strengthen one from within.

One of the largest studies of bereavement experiences was conducted by Susan Nolen-Hoeksema and her team at Stanford University.[4] They studied 300 people across circumstances and time to see how they coped with the death of a dear one.

One of the most common aftereffects on the bereaved was that they gained a greater appreciation of other relationships in their lives. A woman participant elaborated on how the loss made her conscious of how we expend effort on small, insignificant events and waste our energies ruminating on negative feelings.

Tragic loss often unleashes forgiveness and forbearance from the deepest corners of our hearts. The loss of a loved one evokes wisdom regarding the value of life. Realizing its fragility and brevity, one becomes more empathetic when dealing with others.

---

[4] Jonathan Haidt, *The Happiness Hypothesis: Finding Modern Truth in Ancient Wisdom*, New York: Basic Books, 2006, Chapter 7, Kindle e-book.

Further, bereavement forces our inner strength to shine forth. Where we once relied on someone else for our sustenance, we now are mandated to rely on ourselves. This happens to widows who considered themselves as homemakers dependent on their husbands. The sudden demise of their husband propels them to acquire new skills and rise to the occasion.

Altered circumstances make us struggle, which ultimately makes us stronger. This new-found resilience gives us the confidence to face future challenges.

Post-Adversity Growth

Problems make us courageous and wise. Very often, we enter into them with fear and uncertainty. But we emerge from them with renewed faith and wisdom that empower us for the rest of our life. This is termed 'post-traumatic growth' by psychologists, where there is a positive change in behaviour following an adverse experience.

King Ashoka was the third king of the Mauryan Empire, and the grandson of Chandragupta Maurya. He took the Mauryan empire to its greatest heights by usurping many kingdoms using his vast military forces. In his conquest of Kalinga, a coastal kingdom in eastern India, now known as the city of Bhubaneshwar, his army slaughtered lakhs of people.

Although he was victorious, he was seized by remorse and filled with horror at what he had done. He renounced violence and turned to Buddhism.

Carnage, destruction and death caused so much trauma in King Ashoka that it resulted in a profound transformation in him from cruelty to humanity. His kingship was then devoted to nurturing his sprawling empire through non-violence and dharma. His vision of a just society and his rules for virtuous behaviour were carved into rock walls throughout his kingdom. He treated his subjects humanely and even sent delegates beyond the Indian borders to spread his vision of peace.

King Ashoka's restructuring of values and priorities was an example of post-traumatic growth. Following a calamity, people have been known to grow their appreciation for life, become more spiritual, develop new skills and discover new possibilities in life. While the adversity is temporary, the learning is permanent.

Of course, post-adversity growth does not dawn on everyone. In fact, we all have a different threshold or tolerance for adversity. Psychologists have coined the term, Adversity Quotient (AQ), a measure of the capability of an individual to face difficult situations in life. The greater your AQ, the greater your ability to survive and thrive. Let us then discuss how we can increase our adversity quotient and tap into the potential for post-adversity growth.

What We Can Consciously Do to Be Happy during Adversity

Accept adversities as an inevitable part of life. The Universe is full of dualities—day and night, hot and cold, rain and drought. The same rose bush has a beautiful flower and also an ugly thorn. Life too brings its share of opposites—happiness and distress, victory and defeat, fame and notoriety.

Hence, irrespective of the event, the first step is to acknowledge and accept the incident rather than deny or run away from it. Once you make peace with adversity as an integral part of life, only then does a positive reinterpretation of the situation become possible and this in turn paves the path for post-adversity growth.

The Bhagavad Gita states:

*mātrā-sparśhās tu kaunteya śhītoṣhṇa-sukha-duḥkha-dāḥ
āgamāpāyino 'nityās tans-titikṣhasva bhārata*

(verse 2.14)

Shree Krishna explains that the fleeting perceptions of happiness and distress arise because of contact between the senses and the sense objects. These come and go like the winter and summer seasons. We must remember they are not permanent. Thus, we must learn to tolerate them without being disturbed.

Stop imagining greener grass in others' lives. Everyone has their share of problems—no one is spared. Yet, we bring more misery on to ourselves by comparing, as the following story illustrates.

There was a famous sage who lived high up in the Himalayan mountains, far away from civilization. Once, a group of people approached him with their problems. The sage was wise and wanted to teach a lesson. He asked each person to write down their biggest problem on a piece of paper and put it in a common bag. Next, he circulated the bag and asked everyone to pick up one slip. He then calmly stated, 'Read the problem to yourself. You have a choice to own that problem or take back your originally stated problem.'

One by one every person in the group picked out a paper chit, read the other's problems and was horrified. Each concluded that their problem, no matter how bad, was better than the next person's.

While we think happier people have less problems, the reality is quite different. Happy people remind themselves of others who have bigger problems and do not take their own too seriously. So, it is a matter of perspective. Most problems are small in the grand scheme of things. Let that be our mindset!

Be solution-oriented. We spend more time agonizing over a problem and less time on finding a solution to it. Once you have spotted a problem, you must solve it. Many of us get overwhelmed in adverse situations.

We fall prey to anger, anxiety or stress, whereas they could easily be avoided if we simply focused on solutions.

A deer in the forest was pregnant. It found a spot by the river to deliver its baby. However, as the labour pains began, she noticed lightning had set the forest on fire. To her left was an even more fearful sight—a hunter was taking aim at her. But then she noticed even more danger looming. A hungry lion had spotted her and was getting ready for the kill.

The poor deer was cornered from all sides and had nowhere to run. Besides, the labour pains had already begun. She gathered herself together and focused on giving birth to her fawn. In the meantime, lightning struck and blinded the hunter as he released his arrow. He missed his target and the arrow hit the lion. The heavy rains doused the forest fire, and the deer succeeded in giving birth to its fawn.

What is the moral of the story? **When overwhelmed with challenges, remain calm. Focus on what is in your control. Put your best efforts in that direction, leaving the rest in the hands of God.** As the saying goes: 'Do your best and leave to God all the rest.'

God Teaches Us Wisdom through Adversity

Wisdom cannot be taught; it must be experienced. Merely reading about it without its application will not suffice. For example, reading about the various strokes of swimming is helpful. But without practically diving into the water, we cannot become swimmers. Similarly, we may hear lectures of wisdom, but without coping with the vicissitudes of life, we cannot truly become wise. In fact, wisdom that is painfully gained stays fresh and for much longer.

Parents often make the mistake of overprotecting their children. By doing so, they unintentionally hinder their growth. Sheltered children are risk-averse; they have difficulties making decisions and braving hardships. As it is said: 'If we treat children with kid gloves, they grow up as babies.'

God is our perfect parent. He has blessed us with infinite potential. Since it is His desire that we manifest this potential and let His glory shine through, He does not shelter us from adversity. On the contrary, He sends these hard times precisely to make us aware of our shortcomings and eliminate them. Doing so enables our higher self and God's glory to sparkle brightly. You might be familiar with a beautiful poem that goes like this:

I prayed to God for strength; He gave me obstacles to overcome that I may become strong.

I prayed to God for courage; He gave me dangers to surmount that I may become courageous.

I prayed to God for wisdom; He gave me problems to solve that I may become wise.

I prayed to God for love; He gave me the poor and downtrodden to serve that I may develop love.

I received nothing I wanted . . .

I received everything I needed.

In the Vedas, a word for God is Brahman. Jagadguru Shree Kripaluji Maharaj explains the meaning of Brahman:

brahm vṛihatvāt as baṛā jāko ādi na ant
baṛā bṛinhaṇatvāt as, auran kare anant
                                        (*Bhakti Śhatak* verse 51)

This verse states that the definition of Brahman has two parts to it:

1) Brahman is He who is infinitely big. This is evident because God holds innumerable universes within His being.

2) Brahman is He who makes others big.

This second definition of God is of great relevance to us. It implies that the Lord desires His little parts to grow in divine virtues and become perfect like Himself.

The same idea is mentioned in the Bible as well: Be perfect, therefore, as your heavenly Father is perfect. (Matthew 5:48)

Our spiritual Father has built problems into the grand design of the world. It is within His ability to remove them all in an instant. But that would deprive us of the key to spiritual growth. Consider the example of baby eagles.

Eagles fly long distances to gather twigs for their nest, which they make at great heights on mountain cliffs. Once the structure is in place, they carefully pad the inside with cotton and leaves. When the chicks are born in the nest, the mother eagle lovingly nurtures them. But in a few days, the nest becomes overcrowded. The mother instinctively knows that to survive, her young ones will need to leave their nest.

She then begins withdrawing the padding, so the thorns prick the young birds. As the nest becomes painful, they are compelled to climb out. They are now on the cliff's edge, but still too scared to fly.

The mother eagle intervenes again when she decides the time is right. It lures the young ones to the edge and pushes them over. As they begin plunging downwards, they flap their wings to decelerate. In the process, they begin doing what they were destined for. They fly in the skies as the king of birds!

Just as the baby eagles learnt to fly under pressure, God catalyses our growth by pushing us to face adversities.

Have Faith in God's Plan When Things Fall Apart

Sometimes all seems lost and no solution is in sight. It is precisely at this time that we must keep our faith alive and not lose hope in God's goodness. Faith means having the conviction that He is our well-wisher. His plan may not be clear to us, yet we know that it is for our highest good. He can do no wrong and just as parents wish for the best for their children, God too wants the best for us.

One woman was knitting a sweater for her granddaughter. The child ran to her granny to look at the knitting. Seeing the tangled woollen strings hanging haphazardly, she exclaimed, 'This is awful! I cannot wear something like this!'

The grandmother smiled and asked the child to climb into her lap. When the child came over and looked at the knitting from above, she saw a wonderful pattern slowly emerging.

Likewise, from our imperfect perspective, we become baffled in unsettling times. We question if there is any proper order in creation or is it just random chaos? However, when we look at it from the side of the Supreme, there is always a grand design in place. **Difficulties are not meant to kill our spirit, but to help us become our best selves. When we have this faith,** it keeps us strong and gives us the determination to continue.

Saintly Perspective on Adversity

The Bhagavad Gita explains how the perspective of saints differs from others:

yā niśhā sarva-bhūtānāṁ tasyāṁ jāgarti sanyamī
yasyāṁ jāgrati bhūtāni sā niśhā paśhyato muneḥ

(verse 2.69)

'What worldly people consider as day, the saints look upon as night; and what all creatures see as night, the introspective sage sees as day.'

Those in mundane consciousness look to material enjoyment as the real purpose of life. Hence, they consider the opportunity for worldly pleasures as 'day'. Likewise, they see deprivation from sense pleasures as 'night'.

On the other hand, saintly people see sense enjoyment as harmful for the soul, and hence view it as 'night'. They believe refraining from sense objects is elevating to the soul. Thus, they look on it as 'day'.

The saints are convinced the supreme purpose of life is the elevation of our soul. Adverse conditions provide opportunities for spiritual progress. In fact, worldly luxuries are dangerous because they increase our attachment to material things. This is why, Kunti

Devi, mother of the five Pandav brothers, requested hardships from Shree Krishna.

vipadaḥ santu naḥ śhaśhvatatra tatra jagad-guro
bhavato darśhanaṁ yat-syāda-punar-bhava-darśhanam
                        (Shreemad Bhagavatam 1.8.25)

'O Jagadguru Shree Krishna! Please continue to send calamities in my life.' Mother Kunti rejected material comforts. She realized that every time she faced a calamity, she was closer to God.

So, from a higher perspective, adversity is not a bad thing after all. It fills us with real wealth—the treasure of the soul, which is devotion to God.

Take Responsibility for Your Adverse Circumstances

As long as we are under maya, we have accumulated karmas, both good and bad. We bear the fruit of good karmas without a second thought. But when consequences of our bad karmas fall upon us, we become despondent and blame God. Instead, we must also patiently bear the fruit of our misdeeds of endless lives. Then bhakti will become our right.

A beautiful verse in the Bhagavatam explains this:

tat te 'nukapāṁ susamīkṣhamāṇo
bhuñjāna evātma-kritaṁ vipākam

hṛd-vāg-vapurbhir-vidadhan-namas-te
  jīveta yo mukti-pade sa dāya-bhāk (10.14.8)

The verse explains that bhakti is bestowed upon those who fulfil three conditions.

1. *Tat te 'nukampāṁ susamīkṣhamāṇo.* Keep waiting for the divine grace without losing patience. Continue working to make yourself eligible for His grace.

2. *Bhuñjāna evātma-kṛitaṁ vipākam.* Whatever joys and sorrows come into our life are a consequence of our past karmas. Alternatively, they are a direct intervention of God for our spiritual elevation. Accept them serenely as His grace without complaining or accusing the Lord.

3. *Hṛd-vāg-vapurbhir-vidadhan-namas-te.* Keep offering your respects to the Lord with your body, words and mind. Stay positive and devotional.

If you can fulfil these three conditions, you will be granted *parā bhakti* and will be freed from the anguish of maya.

So, whenever adversity comes in life, embrace the opportunities that lie in it. Look for ways to improve and grow. Many people ask me: 'How do I know if I am progressing? What does growth look like?'

Here is a simple answer: '**When there is a reason to be disturbed, but you are not. When there is reason** to be attached, but you are not. When there is reason to be proud, but you are not. When there is reason to be irritated but you are calm.' Hence, the sign of true progress is when you have learnt the art of being happy in adversity.

We will now proceed to learn how to effectively interact with others and cultivate happy relationships.

Summary

- Adverse circumstances are an inevitable part of our life. It is for us to find meaning in unpleasantness and be happy amidst adversity.

- Failure is not necessarily bad. In fact, it can be the raw material for a successful journey ahead.

- Physical pain may be unpleasant, but it has the potential to also save our life.

- Enduring reversals in our profession can propel us to give our best and produce better results.

- Tragic loss such as bereavement can feel overwhelming but can also help manifest positive qualities that were dormant and strengthen one from within.

- Post-adversity growth enables us to appreciate life more, become spiritual and develop new skills.

- We can consciously choose to remain happy during adversity by 1) accepting problems as an inevitable part of our lives; 2) reminding ourselves that others have their own share of problems; and 3) being solution-oriented.

- God uses hard times to make us aware of our shortcomings and eliminate them. In facing negative situations, we become wise. Saints willingly embrace adversity as an opportunity for elevation of the soul.

- We must retain our faith in the midst of a crisis. Just as we reap the results of our actions happily, so too we must patiently bear the fruit of our misdeeds of endless past lives.

6

Happiness in Relationships

Sharing and caring are intrinsically hardwired into the human psyche. We all want to love and be loved. Human exchanges of care and affection are healing and heartening. Empathy and understanding, when shared in relationships, make us feel secure and cared for. People look for a shoulder to lean on as a coping mechanism. The warmth of intimacy creates a beautiful feeling. Hence, we all crave genuine love and authentic heart-to-heart connections with people.

Human connections and interactions play a vital role in our happiness. Since we are social beings, we feel the need to form interpersonal relationships that are strong and stable. And not those on social media; it is the one-to-one personal connections that matter. That is why people say that a good life is built with good relationships.

Let us explore how happiness and relationships are interconnected.

Link between Relationships and Happiness

There is an interesting concept in gardening known as 'companion planting'. It is a practice where certain crops are kept close to one another to help them mutually thrive. For example, corn, pole beans and squash form a symbiotic combination. The corn stalks provide support for the pole beans, which pull nitrogen from the air and bring it to the soil. Meanwhile, squash reduces weeds, shades the soil and helps retain moisture. Together, they assist each other by repelling pests and making the environment conducive to growth. This is why, in gardening, they are called 'Three Sisters'.

This is nature's example of how we can grow stronger together. Similarly, interpersonal bonds are an important component of human needs. These could be forged amidst family, friends or work colleagues. Multiple studies have concluded that people with good social connections are happier, healthier and live longer.[1]

To this effect, social scientists have probed the longevity secret of centenarians (those who have lived

---

[1] Jessica Martino, Jennifer Pegg and Elizabeth Pegg Frates, 'The Connection Prescription: Using the Power of Social Interactions and the Deep Desire for Connectedness to Empower Health and Wellness', *American Journal of Lifestyle Medicine*, Vol. 11, 6, pp. 466–75, 7 October 2015, doi: 10.1177/1559827615608788, https://www.ncbi.nlm.nih.gov/pmc/articles/PMC6125010/.

100 years or more). 'Blue zones' are places on the globe with an exceptionally high ratio of centenarians. Okinawa, in Japan, is one of the five blue zones. Dr Makoto Suzuki started the Okinawa Centenarian Study in 1975.[2] It is the world's longest and continuous study of centenarians.

More than 1000 people over the age of 100 were examined to understand factors responsible for healthy ageing. The study uncovered that the longevity of Okinawans had a strong correlation to their healthy diet and genetics.

Besides these, Okinawans have a strong sense of purpose, based on the Japanese theory of *Ikigai* or 'reason for being'. It keeps them highly motivated and inclined to continue with their job, rather than retire. Instead of sitting idle, they prefer to participate in activities they are passionate about, such as gardening or attending spiritual congregations.

These factors and their correlation with a long lifespan were not surprising. But what came as a surprise was the importance of social bonding. Okinawans notably have strong familial ties and tend to put their family and friends above work. Seniors are revered as assets

---

[2] Kate Whiting, 'Want to Live a Long, Healthy Life? 6 Secrets from Japan's Oldest People', World Economic Forum, 29 September 2021, https://www.weforum.org/agenda/2021/09/japan-okinawa-secret-to-longevity-good-health/.

of the community, which makes them feel valuable and cared for.

The Okinawan Centenarian Study illustrates how strong relationships can induce happiness, better health and long life. The same correlation between human bonding and good health has been validated by a plethora of studies.[3] These have demonstrated that people with high levels of social support have improved immunity markers, lower risk of cardiovascular disease and reduced mental decline. This can be attributed to feeling valued and having people they can trust.

Now, the icing on the cake. Good relationships not only protect your health, but also protect your brain. A research study at Harvard revealed that people in their eighties who had sound relationships displayed sharper memories.[4] Acts of kindness and compassion have proven to flood the brain with the 'happy' hormones, to the extent that hearing phrases, such as 'I love you', can signal the brain to change your heart

---

[3] Jessica Martino, Jennifer Pegg, and Elizabeth Pegg Frates, 'The Connection Prescription: Using the Power of Social Interactions and the Deep Desire for Connectedness to Empower Health and Wellness', *American Journal of Lifestyle Medicine*, Vol. 11, 6, pp. 466–75, 7 October 2015, doi: 10.1177/1559827615608788, https://www.ncbi.nlm.nih.gov/pmc/articles/PMC6125010/.

[4] Zameena Mejia, 'Harvard's Longest Study of Adult Life Reveals How You Can Be Happier and More Successful', CNBC Make It, 31 October 2017, https://www.cnbc.com/2017/10/31/this-harvard-study-reveals-how-you-can-be-happier-and-more-successful.html.

rate, breathing and metabolism. Such studies lend further credibility to the uplifting effects of positive human interactions.

That said, relationships alone do not contribute to happiness and wellness. It is the quality of our close relationships that matters. After all, you can be in a conflict-laden marriage that could be detrimental to health or have many friends yet still be lonely.

Our aim is to invest in positive and nurturing relationships that boost our well-being. Like any endeavour, successful relationships need to be cultivated, which means to nurture them with love and compassion.

Let us first understand what hurts and sabotages our relationships. Then we shall learn the art of cultivating harmonious ones.

Expectations Are the Bane of Relationships

What is the biggest cause for strained relationships? Unfulfilled expectations. 'Why does he not behave like this?' 'Why does she not think like that?' The end result of expectations is invariably dissatisfaction. That is why the saying: 'Expectations are premeditated resentments.'

Expectations are usually about needing the other party to conform to our viewpoint.

The Mughal emperor Akbar's daughter developed pain in her eyes. The hakim (doctor) recommended she see only green to calm them. Akbar commanded his servants to paint everything green in the vicinity of his palace.

Birbal, his trusted minister, was walking into the palace when the servants came with a brush and paint to colour him green as well. Birbal was taken aback and requested a private audience with the king.

'O Badshah, what kind of instruction is this?' asked Birbal.

'My daughter must see only green to heal her eyes. So, I have asked everything be painted green in the vicinity of the palace,' said Akbar.

'But Jahanpanah,' Birbal countered, 'You could do the same in a different way. Just make her wear green glasses. She will then not see any other colour.'

Likewise, we want others' behaviours to match our inclinations and for this we remain agitated. We want to change the whole world, so that we may be peaceful. Instead, if we forsake our expectation, we will find peace.

What are some examples of expectations? Here are some, along with their antidotes.

- **Expecting perfection.** People are human and prone to err. Yet, we grumble and get annoyed at others'

mistakes, claiming they should have known better. If you want peace, let go of unrealistic expectations of perfection from others. Instead, help them overcome their weaknesses by lending support and empathy.

- **Expecting others to do as you wish.** This especially holds true in parent-child relationships. Children *must* be respectful; they *must* be obedient; they *must* get into a top-tier college. These are all unreasonable expectations that may or may not fructify. The same holds true for married couples who constantly argue over things, demanding their way or no way. Instead, maintain harmony by accepting others as they are.

- **Expecting others to desire what you desire.** We all have our own individual likes, interests and goals. One likes movies, while another enjoys reading a good book. Neither is right or wrong, just different. Giving people the freedom to live life on their own terms—while not compromising on collective goals—will bring peace.

- **Expecting others to read your mind.** We forget to communicate our wishes to others, and then expect them to know. For example, a wife gets upset because her husband has come home late but does not tell him so. He sees her in a bad mood but does not have the haziest idea why. Instead, if she had explained her expectations, the chances that the husband apologizes or explains the reason for the delay would be greater.

- **Expecting reciprocation.** This is another very prevalent expectation. For example, you help a friend deal with depression with compassion and care. In exchange, when you need emotional support, you expect the friend to return the favour. If this does not happen, the friendship ends.

Remember that expectations cannot always be fulfilled. Relationships are not contracts—give and take will never be equal. **To be happy, learn to give more than you take, and to love than to be loved.**

Root Cause of Expectations is Selfishness

The underlying cause behind expectations is self-seeking. We want others to give us happiness and satisfaction. The Ramayan states:

sur nar muni sab kī yah rītī, svārath lāgi karahiṅ sab prītī

'Celestial gods, humans and pandits—all have the same nature. Wherever their self-interest is met, they develop affection.'

Sometimes, we point out others' errors and suggest they correct themselves. We think we are pointing out their mistakes for their welfare. The hidden intention, however, is that their behaviour disturbs us, and we need them to change it so it will make us happier. Consider the following story.

A husband and wife began arguing at night. They had quarrelled often in the past, but on this occasion, it took a serious turn. Furious, the husband stomped out of the house and went to sleep in his car parked in the driveway.

An hour later, the wife had a change of heart. She realized how much she loved her husband. As a caring gesture, she took her husband's favourite soda bottle from the fridge and went to the car. Seeing him sleeping, she placed the soda bottle on the dashboard.

She thought that when her husband would wake up, he would be touched to see her loving gesture, and he would also remember how much he loved her. Then they would live happily ever after. Now, had this been a fairy tale, that would have been a probable ending. But this was not a fairy tale; it was real life.

When the husband woke up, his anger had not yet subsided. Seeing the soda bottle on the dashboard, rather than drinking it, he poured it on to the road and then smashed the bottle.

When the wife came to know what the husband had done, she became infuriated. She came to me for counselling, and said, 'Swamiji, I loved him so selflessly. Instead of reciprocating, how could he behave so nastily!'

I gently pointed out to her that if she was expecting a reciprocation, then she was not being as selfless as she claimed.

The fact that the lady got frustrated when her expectation of reciprocation was not met, was an indication of her self-seeking. **If our intentions are genuinely selfless, we will be more accepting, flexible in our attitudes and sacrificing in our dealings.**

Vedic wisdom tells us that until we obtain true happiness, everyone in this material world will remain selfish to lesser or greater degrees. This is natural, not astonishing. If we can become aware of it, we will be propelled to become more selfless in our relationships and reduce our expectations.

We will discuss how to practise selflessness later in the chapter. Let us next learn why it is virtually impossible for two people, let alone a family or a group, to agree all the time.

Changing Gunas

Emotions in relationships can be very complex. They can range from good to bad to ugly. Have you ever wondered why our feelings for one another fluctuate throughout the day? One moment we are on cloud nine thinking the other is an angel. The next moment, our euphoria disappears, and we think the other is a devil.

The scriptures explain with great clarity the science behind strife. The *Shwetāshvatar Upanishad* of the *Yajur Veda* states:

> *ajāmekāṁ lohitaśhuklakṛishṇāṁ*
> *bahvīḥ prajāḥ sṛijamānāṁ sarūpāḥ*
> *ajo hyeko jushamāṇo 'nuśhete*
> *jahātyenāṁ bhuktabhogāmajo 'nyaḥ*   (mantra 4.5)

This Vedic mantra states that maya is of three colours: white, red and black. These correspond to the three gunas (modes): sattva (goodness), rajas (passion) and tamas (ignorance).

Our mind is also made of the material energy, maya, and hence, our temperament fluctuates among the three gunas—sattva, rajas and tamas. When sattva dominates, we are calm, tolerant and empathetic. With rajas as the overruling guna, desires of the senses control us—we crave wealth, power, comfort and the fruits of our actions. Tamas deludes us into anger, laziness and sleep.

Our disposition oscillates among the three gunas throughout the day. Compare them to three wrestlers— sometimes the first drops the second, then the second floors the third, and then the third overpowers the first. Likewise, the battle among the three temperaments continues inside our mind. The prevailing guna at any moment is dependent on: 1) the environment surrounding us; 2) our thoughts; and 3) our *sanskārs* (tendencies from past lives).

Let us say you are listening to words of wisdom on a podcast. Your mind is tranquil while it contemplates divine knowledge. In the meantime, the bell rings—your son has returned from school. You welcome him home with a warm embrace and offer him a tasty midday snack. Your mind is now desirous of reciprocation of love from your son. But instead, you get his wrath. He throws a tantrum—he dislikes the food and runs up to his room. You are infuriated by his reaction and decide to give him a piece of your mind. Your thoughts are now flooded with anger. Within a matter of moments, your gunas changed from good to bad to worse.

Just as your gunas keep changing, the gunas of others also keep changing. Differences in opinion between two people happen when their gunas do not match. Consider couples who do not seem to see eye-to-eye on anything because their state of consciousness differs. The wife wants to attend a spiritual retreat, whereas the husband wants to go on a trip to Las Vegas for the long weekend. Clearly, the wife is dominated by sattva, while the husband is taken over by the rajas guna. Now, conflict begins because of a difference in modes.

Will strife end if the gunas match? Not really.

Let us say both husband and wife are under the influence of rajas and decide to go to Las Vegas. They arrive there, check-in to the hotel, and are ready to head out for a night of fun and frolic. The husband remarks to the wife, 'Let us go to the new casino that has opened.'

The wife, who is a little more refined thinker, says, 'No, I would rather attend the opera at the theatre.' They argue and bicker, finally parting ways to their chosen destination. Though both are in the mode of passion, one has a greater intensity of rajas than the other.

Hopefully, the above scenarios have painted a picture of how these modes influence people at every moment. Conflicting gunas result in a collision of the temperaments. Is it surprising then that others disagree with us? In fact, we should be amazed when others concur with our views! This realistic expectation will free us from a lot of mental strife.

Having understood the reasons for interpersonal conflicts, we will now learn how to nurture our relationships and make them strong and beautiful.

How to Cultivate Happiness in Relationships

1. Build your relationship bank account

We all have checking accounts at the bank. We build them with deposits and deplete them with withdrawals. Similarly, human connections can be viewed as accounts that are nourished with deposits and diminished with withdrawals. Every time we respond with kindness, love and encouragement, we strengthen our bonds. These are deposits.

In contrast, rude behaviour, betrayal or overreacting create a dent in our relationships. They are withdrawals. If deposits outweigh withdrawals, we have happy relations. However, when withdrawals overtake deposits, we unfortunately go into overdraw mode. This is when relationships take a hit—they fall apart and cause dissatisfaction.

Relationship researcher, John Gottman, revealed the 5:1 magic ratio of deposits versus withdrawals for harmony. His study of married couples over many years showed that stable and happy relationships require at least five positive actions for every negative one.[5] This means we need a minimum of five loving gestures to counteract the effects of one negative behaviour. If we can master this art, we will be on our way to fostering happy relationships.

I have detailed this concept in my book, *Golden Rules for Living Your Best Life*. So, we will keep the discussion short here. Let us move on to

---

[5] Travis Dixon, 'Studying Marriage: Gottman's Love Lab and the Four Horsemen of Divorce', IB Psychology, 9 May 2019, https://www.themantic-education.com/ibpsych/2019/05/09/studying-marriage-gottmans-love-lab-and-the-four-horsemen-of-divorce/.

other constructive ways to manifest happiness in relationships.

2. Try to understand others

We all inherently desire to be understood and validated by others. However, we forget our obligation to understand them. Even while listening to others, we do not focus on comprehending their viewpoint, but are planning our response for when they stop speaking. Consider the following example.

A teenager comes home upset and frustrated. The mother cajoles him to talk about his problems. He vents about how college is hard, and he is not enjoying it. Instead of being empathetic, the mother immediately starts a lecture on how important it is for his career and how it will open up avenues for him. The teenager feels disappointed and tells the mother, 'I knew you wouldn't understand!'

Does this sound familiar? It is a common phenomenon.

A husband returns home, exhausted after work. He vents about the stress of his work. Instead of empathizing with his feelings, the wife shares wisdom on the root cause of stress. He gets even more infuriated, which confuses his wife as to why her husband is overreacting.

Why does this happen? The reason is simple. We do not strive to understand someone's thought process and emotions. We are more interested in providing our thoughts, feelings and motives to others. We forget that **the goal is to connect and collaborate with others, not win conversations or sound smart.** That is why it is said: 'Be kind first, be right later.'

I read an interesting account of American Airways, which later became American Airlines. In the 1930s, they experienced a huge rise in customer complaints about misplaced check-in luggage. The CEO deployed his station managers to rectify the situation but did not see much change in the outcome.

He then came up with a plan to make his staff understand the situation from the passengers' viewpoint. He asked all the station managers to fly to the company headquarters for a group meeting. And he ensured that each one lost their luggage. Now they could empathize with the discomfort of their customers when baggage got misplaced. Soon enough, customer service of the airline shot up.

As it is said: 'Put yourself in someone else's shoes.' Empathy is a great tool to help us achieve this. Listen to others attentively. Read their body language. Understand their motives and feelings. Then, without judgement, respond sensitively. The aim must be to help others; sometimes this means simply listening to them and not sharing your opinions.

3. Be responsible for your own happiness

While it is good to have a reliable spouse, parents and colleagues, it is damaging to pin your happiness on them. As discussed earlier, no one can truly match your likes and dislikes. This means that we must not burden others with making us happy, nor should we take it upon ourselves to be responsible for others' bliss. Happiness is always an inside job—we must cultivate it from within.

A couple were newly married. A year later, they undertook a trip to meet relatives. One night, they were at a dinner party hosted by the husband's uncle. The old uncle lovingly asked the wife, 'Does your husband make you happy?'

The husband felt confident that his wife would say 'Yes', because she had never complained in their married life. However, to his dismay, she responded, 'No, my husband does not make me happy.'

While the husband looked stunned, the wife continued, 'My husband does not make me sad either. Whether I am happy or not depends upon me alone and not on anyone else.'

Wasn't she a wise lady! She was taking responsibility for her happiness. The external world of people, things and places will always keep changing. If we pin our happiness to something or someone, we will be on an emotional roller-coaster ride. The wise do not wait for circumstances to be ideal to be happy. They realize the gap between the environment and their response. Thus, taking charge of their thoughts and emotions, they exercise their free will to remain ever joyous.

4. Let go of 'should' and 'shouldn't'

When we harbour unrealistic demands of 'should', 'must' and 'ought to', it strains relationships. To promote harmony, reduce 'should' and become more empathetic. This of course is barring moral and legal injunctions, such as 'Do not steal' or 'Do not hurt others'. However, most of our 'shoulds' do not fall in these categories—they are ill-founded.

- *'He should have known better.'*

- *'She should have returned my call. She is being callous and insincere.'*

- *'The doctor should have spent more time on my diagnosis. He is probably not a good doctor.'*

- *'My son should not throw tantrums because he did not get the gift he wanted.'*

Factually, the source of our 'should' statements boils down to a sense of entitlement. These are all examples of expressing righteousness. There is no universal law that states our every desire will be fulfilled. As you can see, harbouring entitlement leads to disappointment.

When we use 'should' against ourselves, it results in guilt and depression; towards others, it causes anger; and against the world, it leads to frustration. What, then, is the way to give up 'should' and 'shouldn't'? Make a counter argument against them. Here are a few examples.

Should statement: 'My husband should always come home early, so that we can spend quality time together.'

Counter argument: 'His boss requires him to stay late on occasion. He may lose his job if he does not. I understand and will be more supportive.'

Should statement: 'My neighbour always borrows items and never returns them. She should learn to be more mindful and sincere.'

Counter argument: 'With a slew of things to attend to daily, she probably forgets. I can always remind her and get those items back.'

Should statement: 'The waiter should have filled my empty glass with a refill of water when he came by.'

Counter argument: 'He did not intentionally neglect it; he was probably distracted.'

Should statement: 'The plumber should have done a better job. My kitchen faucet has been leaking for two days since he worked on it.'

Counter argument: 'He might have missed something, or the new part could be defective. I will call and explain what happened. I am sure he will fix it.'

The point here is to look at the world from others' perspective. Most times, people are not targeting us with harsh words or actions. They are, in fact, going through their own set of problems. Further, they are doing their best as per their skill set. We just need to appreciate this.

Therefore, **when you see things go wrong, relax. Be lenient with the world and learn to accept things and people the way they are.**

5. Correct yourself, not others

Finding faults with others is so easy. Why? It gives our ego a boost. But doing so puts our relationships at risk of fallouts. Instead, we must dovetail our fault-finding tendency to see our own shortcomings. This requires effort yet is worthwhile and will result in happy relationships. Compare it to removing a splinter, which hurts briefly but results in relief afterwards.

Correcting ourselves is a humbling experience. It saves us from judgement and hypocrisy that harm cherished relationships. It also prevents us from playing tit-for-tat on the grounds of morality, by helping us see value in others' arguments.

Acknowledging our faults further allows for a graceful apology. Or at least gets the ball rolling in that direction. For example, 'I made a mistake when I said, "You never understand." I can see why that may have hurt you.' This defuses the other party, and they are likely to reciprocate with a similar statement. A few such exchanges and the conflict is soon forgotten.

By sincerely correcting ourselves instead of others, we become less biased, more broad-minded and hopefully less argumentative. And simultaneously, we become a better person—a winning proposition for ourselves and our relationships.

6. Practice selflessness

All the above points lead to a very simple conclusion—relationships cannot survive through selfish expectations—they thrive with selflessness. Every requirement and rude behaviour spoils a relationship. Every act of kindness and understanding bolsters it.

What are selfless actions in relationships? It means to put relationships ahead of our rules and conventions; to give more and take less; and to be more accepting than expecting. It means to value others' perspectives

and needs over our own, and to be willing to change ourselves rather than try to change the world. And above all, it means to serve, without expectations of reciprocation, because the opportunity to serve is a reward in and of itself.

The Greeks describe three kinds of love:

Eros: this is the romantic and intimate love between husband-wife or lovers.

Philos: this is warm affection seen in long-standing friendships. It is more selfless than eros, and endowed with the virtues of loyalty, appreciation and sacrifice.

Agape: this is unconditional love—the kind that God has for us. It does not depend on merit. It means to forever give to others. It is selfless, without reason.

A lion was chasing a man in the forest. To save himself, the man climbed up a tree. A bear was also in the tree. The lion said to the bear, 'This man is my fodder. Push him down. Or else, I will shake the tree and bring both of you down.'

'Now that he is in the tree, this man is my guest,' said the bear. 'It is my dharma to protect him.' Annoyed, the lion shook the tree trunk with all his might. But the bear not only hung on to the branch with all his might, but also held on to the man, preventing him from falling to the ground.

It became night-time, and the bear went to sleep. The lion was still waiting below. The man thought to himself, 'If I push the sleeping bear down, the lion will get its fodder and will not come after me.' The man heaved at the bear, who awoke in a jiffy and managed to remain on the branch.

The lion said to the bear, 'This man betrayed you. Now throw him down.'

'He was behaving as per his nature,' responded the bear. 'I will act as per my nature and continue to give him shelter.'

The bear expressed causeless acceptance. If we can cultivate such agape love in our relationships, they will undoubtedly thrive. Though it is a difficult virtue to practise, we can take small steps in this direction. Let us consciously choose the benefit of others while remaining true to our principles and values.

Having discussed such effective techniques for harmonizing relationships, we now come to the final one: do not take worldly relationships too seriously. Kahlil Gibran expressed this very nicely in his book, *The Prophet*.

But let there be spaces in your togetherness,

And let the winds of the heavens dance between you.

Love one another but make not a bond of love.

Let it rather be a moving sea between the shores of your souls.

Fill each other's cup but drink not from one cup.

Give your hearts, but not into each other's keeping.

For only the hand of Life can contain your hearts.

While movies and novels romanticize relationships, the reality is far from it. Not because love is hard work but because we forget the bigger picture. We do not realize that ultimately all our worldly relationships are transient.

Worldly Relationships are Temporary

In endless lifetimes, we souls have been transmigrating from body to body. Just as we have no recollection who the relatives in our past life were, likewise the relatives of this life will also be separated, never to meet again.

Consider a train journey across the country. Two people board from the same station. They strike up a friendship, share their food for the trip and exchange contacts. Having become good friends, they invite one another to their homes in their respective cities. Soon after, the train stops at the first friend's destination. He gathers his luggage and invites the other to get off with him. Though an affectionate offer, the second friend declines as that is not his stop. His ticket is valid till his hometown unlike his friend's, which has now expired.

Similarly, all of us have come with our tickets. We have all been given our time on the planet. We have to leave when our time is up. Neither our spouse, relatives nor friends can stop our departure, however much they may try.

Forty years ago, if you went to Rishikesh, you would find logs floating down the Ganges. The woodcutters would cut logs on the mountainside, and instead of carrying them down, they would throw them into the river. The current would carry the logs down. Occasionally, two logs would join together. They would float, seemingly hand-in-hand, and remain together for many days. In fact, sometimes a plant would begin to grow in their midst. What a beautiful bond had formed between the two! But then they would hit a rock, the two logs would separate, never to see one another again.

The same is true for worldly relationships. We traverse together with people for a short while, only to part ways for eternity. I am reminded of *Buddha's Five Remembrances* elucidated in his sermon, the *Upajjhatthana Sutta*. These are truths he asked his disciples to contemplate on. They reflect the impermanence and frailty of life.

I am of the nature to grow old.

There is no way to escape growing old.

I am of the nature to have ill health.

There is no way to escape ill health.

I am of the nature to die.

There is no way to escape death.

All that is dear to me and everyone I love will change.

There is no way to escape being separated from them.

My actions are my only true belongings.

I cannot escape the consequences of my actions.

They are the ground upon which I stand.

These profound words depict the nature of the world and our relationship with it. Our mental state and karmas alone will accompany us to our next life. However, we forget that everything in this world is transient. We assume bodily relatives will always remain. This fallacy gets us into trouble.

Rabindranath Tagore captured this folly nicely when he said: 'We read the world wrong and say that it deceives us.'[6] We take the ephemeral to be permanent. We forget that material objects and relationships will be left behind upon death. Our eternal relative is God who alone will remain with us lifetime after lifetime.

---

6   Rabindranath Tagore, Quotetab, https://www.quotetab.com/quote/by-rabindranath-tagore/we-read-the-world-wrong-and-say-that-it-deceives-us.

God—Our Only True Relative

The soul is a tiny part of God, and hence, its every relationship is with Him. The Supreme is our Father, Mother, Sister, Brother, Beloved and Friend. The Bhagavad Gita states:

gatir bhartā prabhuḥ sākṣhī nivāsaḥ śharaṇaṁ suhṛit
prabhavaḥ pralayaḥ sthānaṁ nidhānaṁ bījam avyayam
(verse 9.18)

'I am the Supreme Goal of all living beings, and also their Sustainer, Master, Witness, Abode, Shelter and Friend. I am the Origin, End and Resting Place of creation; I am the Repository and Eternal Seed.'

The Shreemad Bhagavatam states:

kṛiṣhṇam-enam-avehi tvam-ātmānam-akhilātmanām
(verse 10.14.55)

'Know Shree Krishna to be the Soul of all the souls in all creation.'

We have a body, and we are the soul that energizes it. Similarly, our soul is the body of God, and He is the Supreme Soul seated within it. If God were to leave us for even a moment, our personality would cease to exist. That is the closeness of our connection with Him.

Secondly, God is all-pervading and resides in every atom of His creation. The *Śhwetāśhvatar Upanishad* states:

eko devaḥ sarvabhūteshu gūḍhaḥ
  sarvavyāpī sarvabhutantarātmā   (verse 6.11)

'There is one God; He is seated in everyone's heart and is everywhere in the world.' Wherever we go, there He is present. Hence, He is incessantly with us.

Thirdly, God is selfless. Worldly love is selfish; it rides the high and low tidal waves. However, God's love does not fluctuate. He loves us causelessly for our welfare. Therefore, the Supreme Lord is our eternal and selfless relative. Our most intimate and closest relationship is with Him alone.

Establishing Our Relationship with God

We forget that God is our eternal and selfless relative. To be truly happy, we need to rekindle our relationship with Him. This will require two things— detaching the mind from the world and attaching the mind to God.

For the first—to detach ourselves from the world— we must repeatedly think of the nature of the world. In the Bhagavad Gita, Shree Krishna said to Arjun:

janma-mṛityu-jarā-vyādhi-duḥkha-doṣhānudarśhanam
(13.9)

'Repeatedly contemplate on the defects of material existence—birth, disease, old age and death.' This *chintan* (revision of knowledge) will solidify the understanding that worldly relationships are ephemeral and help us to detach our mind from them.

Does that mean we must give up our worldly relationships? No! In fact, our relationships flourish when we are detached because we learn to relate to others in the spirit of service—as a well-wisher. We become more accepting than controlling, which is the essence of love.

Jagadguru Kripaluji Maharaj would explain, 'Look upon your children as a nurse does.' The nurse plays with the baby, looks after its needs and treats it with tender care as if it were her own. But the moment her job is done, she walks out from your home to the baby in her next shift. She is not the least bit disturbed, nor does she feel pain in separation from the baby.

The nurse is not attached, and yet, she diligently fulfils her responsibility towards the baby. This allows her to continue serving other babies with the same enthusiasm and care. Thus, while attachment is a bane, detachment is a boon for relationships. It allows for togetherness and nurturing, while retaining our freedom.

Next, we must attach our mind to God. For this, we must firmly decide that we are eternal fragmental parts of the Supreme, and think, 'I am His, and He is mine.' This will awaken our loving devotion towards Him. With this yearning, we must then repeatedly strive to fix our mind upon Him.

Once we revive our eternal connection with the Supreme, material attachments will be replaced by divine love for God.

Sage Narad in his *Bhakti Sutras* states:

yal-labdhvā pumān siddho bhavati amṛito bhavati tṛipto bhavati   (sutra 4)

'Upon attaining bhakti (devotion) for the Lord, one becomes perfect, immortal and satisfied.'

These are the consequences of developing love for God. One achieves perfection of the soul by engaging in devotion—one attains perfect bliss, knowledge and love. One is liberated from the cycle of birth and death and obtains immortality. Lastly, revelling in the infinite nectar of love for God, the soul is supremely content. One enjoys freedom from miseries and relishes perfect peace.

Equally critical to our happiness as relationships, or even more, is the workplace. In fact, people spend more time at work than with their life partner. Hence, we shall next discuss how to make our work experience more fulfilling.

Summary

- Strong relationships can induce happiness, better health and long life. However, we sabotage them by various means.

- Expectations strain relationships. Selfishness is the root cause of expectations. Selflessness makes us more accepting and sacrificing in our dealings.

- We must understand it is virtually impossible for two people to agree all the time. Our disposition oscillates among the three gunas of maya throughout the day—sattva, rajas and tamas. Conflicting gunas results in temperaments colliding, causing strife between two people.

- Human connections can be viewed as accounts that are nourished with deposits and diminished with withdrawals. To nurture relationships, build your relational bank account.

- Try to understand the other's viewpoint. Empathy is a great tool to help us achieve that.

- Be responsible for your happiness. Else you will fall prey to the blame game. Let go of 'should' and 'shouldn't'. Correct yourself, not others.

- Love is of three kinds. Eros is the erotic kind of love. Philos is higher affection as in long-standing friendships. Agape is selfless love. That is the one we must strive for and practise.

- Keep the bigger picture in mind—ultimately, all our worldly relationships are transient. Our eternal and selfless relative is God, who alone will remain with us lifetime after lifetime.

- Establishing our relationship with God requires two things: detaching the mind from the world and attaching the mind to God.

7

Happiness at the Workplace

Most professionals spend one-third of their time at work. This amounts to a total of about 80,000 hours devoted to their career, a very large chunk of time. If it is imbued with joy, it becomes a source of great fulfilment. But if filled with frustration, life becomes a drudgery.

Ideally, everyone should enjoy their job. However, statistics reveal this is not the case. The 2022 Gallup survey[1] determining employee satisfaction across 160 countries found that a significant number of employees are emotionally disconnected at their workplaces:

- A full 60 per cent of employees are 'not engaged', meaning they do just the bare minimum to complete the task at hand but do not manifest their potential.

---

[1] 'State of the Workplace 2022 Report', Gallup, State of the Global Workplace Report—Gallup. Accessed 6 October 2022.

- Nineteen per cent are 'actively disengaged', meaning they are miserable at work. They consistently complain, harbour negativity and undermine the morale of their productive co-workers.

- Only 21 per cent of the employees are 'positively engaged', meaning they are enthusiastic about their work and strive sincerely to make their organization succeed.

Companies seek happy employees, for they are more productive and collaborative. Yet, workers who fit this category are low in supply. Employee unhappiness, therefore, results in trillions of dollars of loss in productivity to organizations globally.[2]

Tony Hsieh, the late former CEO of Zappos, an online shoe retailer, famously pioneered the concept of paying $2000 to new employees to quit, if they were unhappy after their four-week training period. The practice was designed to weed out those with low commitment and passion to safeguard the remaining productive workforce.

Realizing the value of happy workers, companies are investing in creating a joyous work environment. Large multinationals, such as Amazon, SAP and Google have appointed Chief Happiness Officers (CHOs), whose

[2] Ryan Pendell, 'The World's $7.8 Trillion Workplace Problem,' Gallup, 14 June 2022, https://www.gallup.com/workplace/393497/world-trillion-workplace-problem.aspx.

role is to spread positivity among employees and improve morale.

This chapter is dedicated to giving you insights as well as pragmatic tools to be more satisfied at work. And we will conclude the chapter with karm yog—the ultimate science of work that will empower you to work in divine consciousness.

Let us begin with the first question: How does one select a suitable career?

Criteria for Choosing a Fulfilling Career

It is possible you find yourself in the wrong career and feel unmotivated. Again, possibly you may not have a choice to change. But if you are still choosing, here are some principles to keep in mind for making a wise career choice.

- Satisfaction at work comes from what you do on the job from moment-to-moment. Hence, your work must be engaging.

- Choose a career that matches your expertise. A job aligned with your competency will enable you to procure good projects and climb the corporate ladder faster.

- When the learning curve flattens out, the job becomes monotonous. An interesting job is one where there are opportunities to learn new skills and develop yourself.

- Your work must challenge you; boredom sets in if it does not. This is counter-intuitive, and people think an easy job will be a happier one. But to the contrary, stepping outside your comfort zone and taking on demanding projects gives a greater sense of fulfilment.

However, be mindful that work is not so demanding that it causes unmanageable stress.

- Your job must add value to society. Choose a career that will help make a difference to the world through your talents. It will result in greater satisfaction.

- Your career should draw the salary you need to sustain your desired standard of living. You must be able to support your family financially as well as accommodate occasional luxuries.

This is a brief overview of the different aspects to keep in mind when making a career choice. They will get you started on a good footing with a job you enjoy. The next step is to thrive at work. We will now discuss important tools to help you make work enjoyable.

Be Process-Oriented, Not Goal-Oriented

Every job comes with objectives and targets. Outcomes are what ultimately count for most organizations.

This is why much emphasis is laid on achieving goals. No doubt, we must produce results, but we must not tie our happiness to them. A British psychologist, Dr Robert Holden, termed this as 'destination addiction', a preoccupation with the notion that happiness is in the next place—the next project, the next promotion or the next job.[3] The commonly held belief is that happiness lies in the future, 'When I achieve "this" or "that", then I will be happy.' More often than not, this causes frustration and despair. For the sake of reaching the finish line, people do whatever it takes, even at the expense of burnout and other collateral damage.

Fortunately, there is a better way of working blissfully: enjoy the process while striving for your goals. It is not merely about getting to the finish line but also 'how' you get there that matters. Let us understand from the example of the Wright brothers and Samuel Langley.[4] Both had the same goal of creating a flying machine.

Langley had government funding and access to the best minds in the United States. The New York Times *would follow his every move, making him famous*

---

3   Robert Holden, PhD, What is Destination Addiction, robertholden. com, https://www.robertholden.com/blog/what-is-destination-addiction/. Accessed 6 April 2023.

4   Wright Brothers Aeroplane Co., https://www.wright-brothers.org/ General/Museum_Entrance/Museum_Entrance.htm.   Accessed   6 April 2023.

through constant press coverage. Yet, most people have never heard of him today despite the uproar created by the media at that time.

The reason is that all the glory of inventing the aeroplane got cornered by the Wright brothers. They were neither equipped with college education nor had access to a laboratory. However, they loved the process. With utmost enthusiasm and excitement, they experimented from the small bicycle shop they owned.

They flew five times a day and failed as many times. They would carry five sets of spare parts to repair the wreckage. Finally, on 17 December 1903, the Wright brothers successfully took flight for the first time. However, neither the public nor the media was there to experience it. The New York Times *found out a few days later.*

Note the difference between their motivations— Langley was working merely for the rewards of success, whereas the Wright brothers were enjoying the process. This is why, the moment Langley came to know that the first flight was successful, he shut down his research. Had he loved the process, he would have gone to the Wright brothers and said, 'Let me help make the aeroplane even better.' However, he quit the moment he realized there were no lucrative awards left.

Aim for Excellence, Not Perfection

Striving for perfectionism at work is an open invitation for stress. Perfectionists see nothing beyond the goal and achieving it perfectly. Anything less is perceived as failure. This causes unnecessary pressure and anxiety. Their expectations never let them be at peace. It is rare to meet happy perfectionists.

How can we overcome such an attitude? By aiming for excellence rather than perfection. It means doing the best you can do. When we pursue excellence, we strive to do better than before. The race is not with others but against ourselves. With this goal, we keep taking incremental steps to overcome our weaknesses while enhancing our strengths. Each time we fumble and fall in the process, we get up and move ahead.

Pursuing excellence is about continuous improvement, not about any single accomplishment. Since the objective is progress, whatever be the results, we feel a sense of fulfilment for having put in our best effort. How different is this from an attitude of perfectionism!

Leverage Humour at Work

The corporate world can be very dry. People can get obsessed with propriety and keep a tight rein over their emotions. Many even believe that success and humour are at opposite ends of the spectrum. However, this is far from the truth.

People who use humour at work are less stressed, more productive and more cheerful. Studies reveal that leaders with a sense of humour are 27 per cent more liked than grim bosses. Their employees are 15 per cent more engaged and their teams perform better.[5] Humour boosts perceptions of confidence and competence. Levity helps the audience see the other person's authentic side, the real deal. It is a great trust-builder.

Hence, humour contributes significantly to success at work. Communication delivered with a touch of humour is more impactful. Your emails and presentations are better received when you add a little hilarity. Also, humour fires neurons in the brain that release serotonin. The resultant feeling of happiness brings out your creative side and aids in learning.

Laughter acts as a social lubricant. It helps form meaningful relationships at work through positive experiences. This leads to team cohesiveness and agreement around group targets. Joviality can also be a great tool to diffuse workplace tension. Here is a funny story for you.

---

[5] Jennifer Aaker and Naomi Bagdonas, 'How to Be Funny at Work,' *Harvard Business Review*, 5 February 2021, https://hbr.org/2021/02/how-to-be-funny-at-work.

Connor Diemand-Yauman, the co-CEO of a large non-profit organization called Merit America, was leading his company's first virtual offsite meeting during the lockdown. Connor shared a few slides before handing over to another teammate to speak. During the transition, he intentionally continued to screen-share while opening up Google search. While most people would have interpreted this as a typical virtual accident, Connor typed in 'Things inspirational CEOs say during hard times.' Everyone ended up laughing. It eased all prevailing tensions.

Since we spend one-third of our lives at work, why not make the experience more enjoyable by adding humour? You may feel you lack levity, but it is simpler than you think. Like other skills, humour too can be learnt. Here are some ways to practise it at work:

- *Laugh at yourself, and make others laugh alongside.*

- *Smile often, and make others smile back in response.*

- *Create a collection of funny jokes. Share with colleagues at appropriate moments.*

- *Read funny cartoons or quotations. Post them on bulletin boards.*

- *Surround yourself with people who have a sense of humour.*

- *Begin meetings with the narration of a humorous incident.*

It is not about making situations at work funny, rather making work more fun. A little bit of light-heartedness breaks the monotony of work and increases everyone's satisfaction.

How to Thrive in a Job You Do Not Love

Every work comes as a mixed bag, and every job has its annoying aspects. It may require performing boring tasks or dealing with irritating colleagues, but you have to learn to thrive regardless. Here are a few suggestions.

Build meaningful relationships at work. Having a trusted colleague—whom you can confide in and gain perspective from—can be a great stress reliever. A confidante at the workplace can motivate you through rough times.

Focus on the positives in your job. Though you may not enjoy your role, shift your attention to the good things about your work environment. Possibly, you could appreciate the constructive company culture. Or perhaps you could be thankful that working hours allow for work-life balance. Or simply feel gratitude that you have a job. Such positive reframing will do wonders for your happiness.

Build skills for your next position. Focus on preparing yourself for the role you have envisioned. Gain support from mentors and take up courses to upskill. Focusing on self-growth will keep you enthused.

Focus on learning from the problematic situation. Even a bad boss can teach you what to do differently when you get a chance to take up a leadership role yourself. If the organization has a poor work culture, focus on how it forces you to become emotionally resilient to survive. Remember, **learning through negative experiences comes more easily than through positive ones.**

We now come to the most important point related to happiness at the workplace.

Achieve Flow in Your Work

No matter what kind of a job you do, would it not be great to be so absorbed in your work that you do not look at the clock any more? This is a state in which your mind is free from distractions, not overwhelmed by stress, but simply immersed in the task at hand.

Some may shrug it off, saying, 'This is not realistic. Work only oscillates between drudgery and demands—it is hardly ever enjoyable or absorbing.' Know that it is possible to achieve such a state of complete absorption, also known as 'flow'.

The concept of flow was popularized by psychologist and happiness researcher, Mihály Csíkszentmihályi.

He studied people and their moods at different times in the workday, by giving them each a pager. The pager would beep several times during the day. The participants had to note down what they were doing at that time and how much they enjoyed it.

Csíkszentmihályi noted that people definitely enjoy low-value fun activities, such as snacking and social interactions. However, his big discovery was that there is a state people value even more. It is when they are completely immersed in a task that is challenging, yet closely matched to their abilities. It is popularly termed 'being in the zone'.

He called it 'flow' because it often feels like effortless movement. For example, flow can occur during speedy driving on a curvy country road, or while having an intense conversation or while playing team sports. Flow can also result during solitary creative activities, such as painting, writing and practising music. The story is told about Ramakrishna Paramhansa.

One day, Ramakrishna Paramhansa came from Dakshineshwar to Kolkata to take part in the Rath Yatra of Lord Jagannath. However, by the time he reached the route, the procession had already moved ahead. He inquired about the Rath Yatra from a painter in a shop. The painter was busy with his artwork. He said he had not seen any procession. A nearby shopkeeper got angry and scolded him for lying to such an elevated saint.

Shree Ramakrishna closed his eyes, went into samadhi and saw that the procession had indeed gone by. The painter had been so absorbed in his artwork that his mind had shut out the entire world, including thousands of people and their tumultuous sounds.

The painter was 'in the zone', or as per the terminology of Csíkszentmihályi, he had demonstrated an exemplary state of flow.

In the flow experience, the subconscious and conscious mind are in harmony. The subconscious is doing most of the work, while the conscious mind is completely absorbed in looking out for problems and opportunities. As per Csíkszentmihályi: 'The best moments usually occur when a person's mind is stretched to its limits . . . to accomplish something difficult and worthwhile.'

Here are the conditions that can get you into the state:

- *The work must be meaningful and aligned with your values. The sense of purpose is important to bring out your best.*

- *The work must be challenging enough to entice your brain. But it should not be so difficult that it completely stresses you out.*

- *You must avoid distractions and fully focus on the task at hand. Turn off your phone, TV and all other allurements.*

- *There should be constant feedback informing you of how you are doing. For example, if a musician is creating a melody, the feedback comes when the notes fall into the proper place. The inner feeling says it was a job well done.*

Achieving flow can considerably improve the quality of our work. It leads to increased concentration, peak performance and creativity. People who frequently experience this state do not get bored, nor do they have time for office politics or gossip. No wonder flow results in happiness!

Now let's learn about managing one of the most important distractions—stress, which prevents us from achieving a state of flow.

Burst the Stress Bubble by Detaching from Outcomes

The modern-day workplace is notorious for the stress it generates in employees. Corporations have introduced many workplace wellness policies, such as flexible hours and indoor games to help ease employee stress. However, all these techniques have short-lived effects. If we wish to be stress-free, we must understand the true source.

People incorrectly link hard work with emotional stress. Let me assure you that toiling hard is not the cause of stress. You can work from morning till night and yet be completely blissful. In fact, modern neurological science tells us that when we work hard, our brain secretes serotonin, making us feel fulfilled. So, stress is not a result of hard work. Then what is the origin of stress and why does it develop?

Stress develops because of our mindset. The former American football player, Lou Holtz, put it nicely, 'It's not the load that breaks you down. It's the way you carry it.'

So, what is the mindset that causes stress? When we are attached to a particular outcome and worried that things may not turn out as we desire, we become anxious.

- *If a businessperson wants to make profits, but fears losses, he experiences stress.*

- *If a sales representative wishes to meet a particular sales target, but apprehends failure, strain ensues.*

- *School students often suffer anxiety near exams. The nervousness is not because they have to study hard but from worry about the results.*

- *Similarly, people often lose their poise when speaking to an audience. What causes stage fright? Their attachment to their self-image, 'Will I look good in the eyes of others?', 'Will my self-esteem remain intact?', and so on.*

In all these cases, the mind clings to outcomes. Thus, **the cause of stress is our attachment to a particular result and our unwillingness to accept other possible outcomes.** Attachment comes with the strong urge to control circumstances. However, the results of our actions are not in our control. They are dependent on several factors, such as circumstances, others' efforts, luck, combined karma of the place, coincidence and God's will, among others.

We must shift our focus to what is in our control—which is our effort. Thus, wisdom demands that we do our duty to the best of our ability and leave the results in the hands of God. This is the secret to working without stress. The Bhagavad Gita gives us the solution to stress in this popular verse:

karmaṇy-evādhikāras te mā phaleṣhu kadāchana (2.47)

'You have a right to perform your work, but you are not entitled to the fruits of your actions.'

This leads to the question: 'How will I achieve my goals if I am not attached to the outcomes? Will that not make me mediocre at my job?'

No, it will not; on the contrary, you will be able to do your job even better. Do not mistake detachment to mean disregard towards work. Nor does it mean reducing your standard of work. Healthy detachment means the reverse. We immerse ourselves in the task at hand and utilize our talents to the utmost. Yet, we do not cling to the desired outcome. This objectivity not only saves us from frustration and nervousness but also gives us clarity of thought and the ability to make wise choices.

You will notice that surgeons do not operate on their own family members. It is not because they are not competent enough or care less for their kin. Rather, they are aware that while operating on a close relative, their attachment can distort the intellect and cause them to make a mistake. Hence, they prefer their colleagues perform the surgery. Likewise, athletes realize if they lose their cool, they are prone to error in the middle of a match. Thus, detachment helps us perform better. Putting aside our emotions allows us to focus on our best effort.

The next question that arises is, 'How do we give up attachment to outcomes?' For this, we must learn the practice of karm yog. Let us learn about it in the following section.

Karm Yog—Working for the Pleasure of God

Most people work with an agitated mind. While they engage their body in the task at hand, their mind harbours sentiments, such as fear, envy, resentment and lamentation. This is a far cry from the state of flow previously discussed. The principle of karm yog aims to change this and empowers us to work from positivity instead of negativity. Let us understand how.

Karm is 'work' and yog is 'union'. Hence, karm yog means to keep the mind in God alongside with doing our work. Simply put, karm yog means 'mind in God, body in the world'.

The Bhagavad Gita tells us how to perform karm yog:

sarveṣhu kāleṣhu mām anusmara yudhya cha   (verse 8.7)

'Remember Me at all times and continue to work.'

The concept of karm yog is usually misunderstood. People think they will be karm yogis if they do an hour of yoga in the morning and work during the day. However, true karm yog is when we do both simultaneously. Our mind must be absorbed in God alongside with doing our worldly duties. Then the mind will remain in divine consciousness.

In karm yog, we do not divide our activities, thinking 'This work is for me, and this is for my Lord.' Rather, we do all our work for the pleasure of God, as service to Him. With such practice, all actions become an offering at the altar of the Supreme. Shree Krishna explains this in the Bhagavad Gita:

yat karoṣhi yad aśhnāsi yaj juhoṣhi dadāsi yat
yat tapasyasi kaunteya tat kuruṣhva mad-arpaṇam

(verse 9.27)

'Whatever you do, whatever you eat, whatever sacrifices you perform, whatever you give away in charity, and whatever austerities you undertake, do them all as an offering unto Me.'

Consider some examples of work in the spirit of karm yog.

- *Earning money is a mundane act. But the same can be done in the mood of devotion. Think thus, 'I will take care of my family with my earnings, so they can engage in bhakti. After that, whatever I save, I will donate in the service of God. Hence, the money I earn is all for the pleasure of God.'*

- *Physical exercise is bodily work. But you can also do it in divine consciousness by thinking, 'I can only serve God with this material body granted to me. So let me exercise sincerely to stay physically and mentally fit.'*

- *While taking care of family members, do so with the intention that they are all children of God, and you are taking care of them for His pleasure.*

With practice, you will gain success in constantly bringing God into every activity and perfect the art of karm yog. When we view our work as service to God, we benefit in many ways:

- *Our work turns from drudgery to joy.*

- *We become motivated to pursue excellence since our intention becomes to please God.*

- *The results are for the pleasure of God, and hence, we become detached from them. We do not feel stressed if we do not get the desired outcome.*

- *When we work in divine consciousness, we see everyone as divine souls. Hence, we do not harbour negative emotions towards anyone.*

- *We develop a deep sense of purpose behind every activity. It is no longer mundane work, rather, a divine service.*

So, how do we achieve the state of constant remembrance of God?

Practise Feeling the Presence of God

Most of us know the art of developing divine consciousness whenever we wish to do so. For example, when we go to the temple, we feel, 'God is present here. I must not think bad thoughts.' This idea makes us reverential. However, when we walk out of the temple, we think, 'There is no God here. So, I can think whatever I like, and nobody will know.' But we forget that God is always sitting within and noting our every thought.

Karm yog corrects this faulty notion by doing a bypass surgery of our consciousness. The technique for accomplishing this is the practise of the presence of God. Presently, we are constantly aware of the self,

'I am'—'I am reading', 'I am writing', 'I am hungry', 'I am full', and so on. However, we forget that God is also always present with us. The scriptures state that He is sitting in our heart as the Supreme Soul. We need to bring this fact in our conscious awareness.

For example, while at work, place God in the seat next to yours. Feel His presence for a moment and then begin your work. After an hour, stop your work and think, 'God is watching me.' Keep the practice going.

Once you are adept at remembering Him after every hour, increase the frequency to every half hour, 'Shree Krishna is with me.' And then every fifteen minutes, 'My Lord is watching me.' With constant practice, the stage will be reached where you will continuously feel the presence of God with you.

We have had many great karm yogis in history. Dhruv, Prahlad and Yudhishthir were all great kings in history. They performed complex tasks and dealt with the problems of their citizens. Yet, while doing all this, they were without a tinge of stress. Their consciousness was constantly absorbed in God.

There is an added advantage of constant remembrance of God. When the mind is attached to the All-pure, it gets cleansed. To the degree it becomes purified, to that extent we become free from anger, greed, anxiety and stress. Hence, if we can succeed in attaching our mind to God, we will be at peace while performing any work in any situation. Only then will we be considered as true karm yogis.

Through the chapters of the book, we have learnt how to be happy in various situations and facets of life. These tools have the potential to vastly enrich your life with joy and a sense of purpose. The next fascinating topic is the neurology of happiness. We can, in fact, induce the onset of chemicals in the brain that make us happy through our thoughts and lifestyle habits. In the next chapter, let's learn the science of happiness.

Summary

- Being happy at work is important to our well-being and career growth.

- While most people are goal-oriented, there is a better way of working blissfully—enjoying the process while striving for your goals.

- Do not sabotage your joy by pursuing perfection. Instead, aim for excellence in all you do.

- Leverage humour at work. It is a great relationship-builder and helps diffuse tension within teams.

- We can thrive in a job we do not love by focusing on the positives and improving our skills for the next role we would like to step into.

- Work becomes sheer joy when you become completely absorbed in it. This is known as the state of 'flow'.

- To be stress-free, we must eradicate it from the root—give up attachment to the outcome of our actions.

- Learn to work in higher consciousness by practising karm yog. This means doing your worldly duties with the body while the mind is absorbed in loving remembrance of God. In such karm yog, you consecrate all your works for the pleasure of God.

- The best way to remember God constantly is to practise feeling His presence at all times.

8

Neurology of Happiness

We think of people as being happy based on their externals—a smile on their face, a large house, a loving family, and so on. However, the brain inside has a bigger role to play than the externals. From a neurological standpoint, we can programme the brain to create feelings of joy and happiness by leveraging its inner workings.

Recent advances in neurology and biotechnology have provided us with tools to study what goes on in the brain. Imaging machines have been developed, such as Magnetic Resonance Imaging (MRI) and Positron Emission Tomography (PET), which are used in conjunction with brainwave analysis technologies, such as Quantitative Electroencephalography (QEEG), also known as brain mapping. The newfound linkages between the mind and the brain show us amazing possibilities of how we can train our neural machinery to cultivate happiness.

Simple habits can rewire our brain and enable us to experience euphoria. This chapter will help you understand the brain chemicals that induce happiness and how to harness their potential. So, let us dig in.

Brain Chemicals

Think of the human brain as a factory that generates chemicals. Different events and our perception of them trigger the release of these chemicals. However, we can reverse the chain of events. We can intentionally trigger their release by what we think and do, thereby generating happiness for ourselves.

The feeling of 'happiness' is particularly connected with four neurotransmitters generated by various parts of the brain. These are the DOSE chemicals: Dopamine, Oxytocin, Serotonin and Endorphins. All four neurotransmitters are powerful. Each one produces a different kind of happiness. Let us explore each one and utilize the knowledge to become more cheerful.

Endorphins

These are our body's natural painkillers. 'Endo' means internal, while 'morphine' is an opiate pain reliever. Hence, endorphin is an 'internally generated analgesic'. The release of endorphins makes us feel energetic, similar to the sensation after an adrenaline rush.

A rush of endorphins can be triggered by various things. Rigorous exercise can trigger the brain to release endorphins. This masks the pain and enables us to continue stretching our limits while exercising. Similarly, marathoners experience a 'runner's high'. Endorphins reduce the perception of soreness. They also promote feelings of pleasure and reduce inflammation caused by injury.

A reduced level of endorphins inhibits positive emotions. It can increase aches and pains and make us moody. Physical exercise and laughter are the easiest methods to facilitate endorphin release. Listening to light music or spending time with friends will also produce it.

Oxytocin

This is the social bonding chemical produced in the hypothalamus of the brain. Oxytocin generates feelings of closeness and trust. It promotes positive social emotions, such as generosity and compassion. It also plays a crucial role in birthing and maternal affection.

Social proximity, hugging a loved one or even a tender touch prompt the release of oxytocin. When you are happy, you are likely to interact positively with others. These positive exchanges engender greater bonding and trust.

Oxytocin is released every time you connect with kindness to an individual or group. When the caring interaction is repeated with a particular individual, the brain gets wired to think positively towards that person over time. This is how oxytocin encourages positive social behaviour in both personal and professional life.

Oxytocin is also called the 'love' chemical because it increases the trust and attraction between people. It could be partially responsible for the phenomenon of 'love at first sight'.

Dopamine

This is the neurotransmitter that creates links in the brain between activities and pleasure. It is released when we contemplate activities that provided pleasure in the past. It is also released when we believe an activity will give pleasure, though we may not yet have engaged in it. Dopamine promises the brain future pleasure. The anticipation of happiness from a particular action becomes the motivation for engaging in it.

For example, reading a new email provides a tiny burst of pleasure. Subsequently, when you get a notification on your phone—indicating arrival of an email—dopamine is released, making you anticipate pleasure from reading it. Hence, it is an excitatory chemical. The problem is that the kick from dopamine is temporary, and it keeps prodding or nudging us to look for the next pleasurable pursuit.

Dopamine differs from most other neurotransmitters. Though it is an excitatory chemical, it can have a two-sided effect. It encourages activities that are pleasurable, but not necessarily good for us, such as indulging in junk food. On the other hand, it can prevent us from engaging in actions that are beneficial but are unpleasurable, such as daily exercise.

If not managed properly, dopamine-inducing activities can turn detrimental. Drinking, gambling, video games or even using social media trigger dopamine's excitatory effects. The pleasurable experience stimulates us to continue the activity, eventually leading to addiction. Then, just to get another hit, we can even squander away our resources and sacrifice our relationships. Dopamine can be highly destructive if not managed properly.

Serotonin

Serotonin is one of the most important neurotransmitters for good mood. It is produced mostly in the gut and partly in the brain. It regulates sleep, appetite and mood. It produces a calming effect, and hence, is powerful in fighting depression and reducing anxiety. In fact, most modern anti-depressant drugs act by increasing the amount of serotonin available to brain cells. Augmented serotonin levels uplift our mood.

Serotonin does not require an external object for its release. It is produced when we feel good about ourselves. This happens when we strive to improve and be the best version of ourselves. Serotonin is also produced when we feel fulfilled about a task well accomplished, or when we recall past accomplishments, such as getting an A in school, or being recognized by the vice president for a job well done or working on a do-it-yourself project that is appreciated by everyone. These small achievements were fulfilling. They gave you a sense of inner satisfaction that was long-lasting, unlike the dopamine kick, which wore off right after the activity was over.

Serotonin is also what gives us a sense of satisfaction when we help others. We all can gain inspiration from Captain Mulla, an Indian Navy officer who was in command of INS Khukri in the Arabian Sea during the Indo-Pak conflict of 1971.

On the night of 9 December 1971, the INS Khukri was hit by torpedoes, and it started sinking. Captain Mulla gave immediate orders to abandon the ship and supervised the arrangements for the rescue of his crew and men on board. In a very calm and methodical manner, he continued to direct rescue operations without any regard for his personal safety.

When life-saving equipment fell short, Captain Mulla gave away his own life jacket to a young sailor. Having directed as many of his men as possible to abandon the ship, he remained undeterred, sat on the bridge and began smoking a cigarette. Those who survived saw the sight of their forty-five-year-old captain calmly puffing on his cigarette as he went down with his ship. His dedication, exemplary gallantry and selfless service to his team and motherland are honoured to date.

The armed forces are full of real-life stories of extraordinary courage and leadership. Why do you think these heroes risk their lives to save others? A significant part of the answer lies in serotonin production in the human body. This is what gives us a sense of deep fulfilment for having positively impacted others.

The brain promotes people to engage in activities that make them feel good about themselves by facilitating the release of serotonin. It is the brain chemical that induces us to 'do good' and 'be good', and through these, truly 'feel good'.

On the other hand, low levels of serotonin cause loneliness and depression. This is also one of the reasons why people engage in harmful attention-seeking activities, such as crimes.

At the physiological level, regular exposure to the sun is another effective way to enhance our serotonin levels. When our eyes perceive sunlight, it stimulates some parts of the retina, which cue our brain to produce serotonin. Bear in mind that exposure to the sun must not be overdone.

I hope this discussion has triggered some happy hormones in you by now. Though these are technical terms, they give us great insights into how we can mould our behaviour to feel happier. Let us continue to explore the physiology of the brain and its connection with happiness.

Biology of the Human Brain

The circuitry of the human brain is complex. However, for the purpose of this chapter, we shall limit this discussion to comprehending its link with the emotion of happiness. For this, the relevant structures and their brief functions are given below. They usually work in tandem to generate emotions and also drive behaviour. Whenever we do any physical or mental work, our brain fires neurons in corresponding regions.

Neocortex: This is the upper part of the brain and is found to be disproportionately large in humans. The neocortex has four large lobes: frontal, parietal, temporal and occipital. The frontal lobes are primarily involved in higher-level thinking and emotions.

Limbic cortex: Located in the central area of the brain, it impacts our moods, motivation levels and judgements. It also plays a key role in decoding our emotions. Increased limbic metabolism is linked to depression tendencies.

Hypothalamus: This is responsible for our emotional responses and hormone release in the body. It also regulates body temperature.

Hippocampus: This helps preserve and retrieve memories. It also plays a role in how intelligently we perceive our environment.

Amygdala: This helps coordinate responses to triggers in our environment, especially the emotions of fear and anger.

Insula: Also called the insular cortex, it is located between the lobes as a separator and is responsible for sensory processing, decision-making and motor control.

An interesting finding of the research[1] done by Dr Richard Davidson, professor at the University of Wisconsin, has shown the correlation between the limbic system and frontal lobes. He demonstrated that the left side of the frontal lobe is more active when people feel happy. It is popularly known as the 'feel

---

[1] Richard J. Davidson and Brianna S. Schuyler, 'Neuroscience of Happiness', World Happiness Report 2015, https://centerhealthyminds.org/assets/files-publications/Davidson-Neuroscience-of-happiness.pdf. Accessed 11 August 2022.

good' centre of the brain. In contrast, the right side of the frontal lobe is more active when people feel sad.

Thus, by learning what stimulates the left prefrontal cortex we can train people to be happier. Similarly, by learning what calms the activity in the right prefrontal cortex we can train people to reduce their sadness.

Further, negativity such as fear or anxiety can activate the amygdala. This causes a release of stress hormones, resulting in an increase in heartbeat, blood pressure and blood sugar. If the amygdala recovery from a threat is slow, it can result in a variety of health conditions.

Certain kinds of training can alter brain circuits and strengthen the left prefrontal cortex to promote positive responses. These include frequently harbouring happy thoughts, not entertaining unproductive thoughts and engaging in healthy behaviour. The key is to repeatedly practice these. Our brain can turn any behaviour into a habit because of its neuroplastic nature. Let us explore that next.

Neuroplasticity—Our Brain's Potential for Growth

Our thoughts create electrical currents that travel from neuron to neuron. Repeated activation of certain neurons creates a neural pathway. This means the more we perform a particular action or think a certain thought, the corresponding neurons form neural highways in the brain. That is why neuroscience has a famous saying: 'Neurons which fire together also wire together.'

The stronger the neural pathway, the faster the message travels and the deeper it gets etched in the brain. The brain further simplifies its work by creating shortcuts to these pathways. Consequently, repeated thoughts and behaviour come more easily to us. This leads to the formation of long-term habits and attitudes. For example, if someone repeatedly brings the emotion of positivity, a corresponding neural pathway gets created where the sentiments of positivity come more easily.

Neuroscientist, Eleanor Maguire, demonstrated the plasticity of the hippocampus as a result of changes in environmental factors.[2] She studied taxicab drivers in London. Their MRI scans showed they had substantially bigger hippocampi than the average person. Why so?

The hippocampus in the brain is responsible for visuo-spatial memory. And the city of London is notorious for its thousands of crisscrossing streets.

---

[2] Ferris Jabr, 'Cache Cab: Taxi Drivers' Brains Grow to Navigate London's Streets', *Scientific American*, 8 December 2011, https://www.scientificamerican.com/article/london-taxi-memory/.

Cab drivers are first trained to navigate its maze-like streets and remember the landmarks, without using maps. By repeated usage, they develop their visuo-spatial awareness and memory, resulting in enlargement of the area of the brain corresponding to that particular skill.

The ability of the human brain to grow new neural connections with changing experiences is not restricted to driving on the twisting streets of London. We too can use it to rewire our brain to feel happier.

Techniques to Rewire Your Brain

There are tangible ways to harness the neuroplastic nature of our brains for increasing our level of happiness. These can be used to consciously enhance 'feel good' chemicals in the brain and volumize areas responsible for happiness.

Try the following daily activities for activating important regions such as the left prefrontal cortex, insula and hippocampus, as well as to decrease the activity of the amygdala:

Meditate. Meditation is a powerful method for changing the physical structure of the brain. It strengthens the prefrontal cortex and insula. This results in higher attention power, sensory processing and self-awareness. As a result, meditators gain control over lower impulses and develop better focus. They also experience less loss of age-related brain cells.

Meditation switches off the stress response of the amygdala and brings it back into balance. This is why a smaller amygdala is noticed in people who meditate regularly.

Meditation increases gamma waves that induce feelings of bliss. It also decreases beta waves, which are prevalent in our waking state, evoking relaxation. Further, both alpha and theta wave patterns are observed during meditation. The presence of these signals that a person is alert yet fully rested in the meditative state. Meditation is an excellent tool to reshape the brain. It facilitates long-lasting positive alterations of the brain.

Apart from improving mental health, it also makes our body healthy. It is known to reduce inflammation, chronic pain, hypertension and a myriad of other health ailments. Consistent practice of meditation bestows inner serenity and contentment.

Exercise. Like the mental exercise of meditation, engaging in physical exercise can strengthen the feel-good centres of the brain. It also lowers cortisol levels, thereby reducing stress. Try exercising in new and different ways to naturally stimulate the release of happy chemicals in the body. Exercise-induced release of endorphins will keep you motivated, and serotonin will enhance your mood.

Be grateful. After love, gratitude is the second most satisfying sentiment. Regularly counting your blessings strengthens those neural connections and makes gratitude a habit. This brings about optimism and joy because it shifts your focus from negative to positive emotions. It activates the release of positive brain chemicals.

Make it a point to thank God for at least three things every day. Think of all the things you could not have been happy without. Or perhaps, think of the small goals you accomplished today. You could say them mentally, or even better, write them in a gratitude journal. You can refer to the journal every time you hit a rough patch in life and rejoice in the abundance that you have.

Positive social interaction. Interacting with others is a basic necessity. Spending time with loved ones and celebrating accomplishments stimulates the hippocampus. It converts social interactions into feelings of happiness and stores them as memories. When you recollect such memories, you repeat your experience of happiness. All this stimulates the left prefrontal cortex.

Play. Nurture the child in your heart by playing games, spending time in nature or on a hobby, or just letting down your guard. In these simple activities, your natural self is not bound by the many made-up norms and regulations of society. Of course, you need to be in a safe, non-judgemental environment to do so. Spending time with children can also bring out your spirited side.

Laugh. Laughter is healing. People with a sense of humour tend to be healthier and happier. Laughing increases the production of endorphins and dopamine. It lowers cortisol levels and opens the learning centres of the brain, making us more creative.

Norman Cousins, an American journalist, used laughter as medicine. He was diagnosed with ankylosing spondylitis, a severe, degenerative, life-threatening disease. At its peak, the illness had paralysed him to the extent that he could not even move his jaw. Despite his doctor sharing that only one out of five hundred people recover from this affliction, Cousins was determined to beat the odds.

He realized that negative thoughts cause illness and hypothesized that positive thoughts can create wellness. Cousins dedicated himself to laughing his way through his illness. He watched all the funny movies he could find, read funny books and heard jokes. Not only was he cured but he also lived to the age of seventy-five with minimal pain.

So, ensure you get your share of laughter daily. Even if you do not feel like it, laugh anyway. Your body still produces the happy chemicals from which you will benefit. You can read more about this in my book, *Golden Rules for Living Your Best Life*, in which one chapter has been dedicated to this topic.

Give. Giving to others impacts our brain in many positive ways. It stimulates our brain's 'reward regions', thereby secreting serotonin and oxytocin. When the brain activity of people giving in charity was tracked, it showed a 'warm glow', which lasts longer than the gratification we feel when we buy material goods. It is often referred to as the 'helper's high' and is addictive like all other highs. Altruism is also known to lower stress and increase longevity. So, simple acts of kindness or even gifting to others makes us feel happier and healthier.

This brings us to the next topic, generosity. Cultivating a big heart to help others is one of the most satisfying behaviours one can engage in. Undoubtedly, it increases our happiness and that of others. Let us dive into it in the next chapter.

Summary

- The feeling of 'happiness' is particularly connected with four neurotransmitters—dopamine, oxytocin, serotonin and endorphins.

- To become happy, we can intentionally trigger their release by engaging in suitable activities and thoughts.

- Endorphins are our body's natural analgesic or painkillers. The release of endorphins makes us feel energetic.

- Oxytocin generates feelings of closeness and trust. Falling in love or hugging a loved one prompts the release of the 'love chemical'.

- Dopamine is an excitatory brain chemical. It is released when you are anticipating pleasure from an activity. It links sensory objects with pleasure in the brain. This leads to more desires for the same and even addiction.

- Serotonin is produced when we do something good and feel fulfilled at a task well accomplished. It gives a sense of lasting satisfaction.

- Strong neural pathways get formed the more we think certain thoughts or perform particular actions. We can rewire our brain to feel happier through neuroplasticity.

- Some techniques to rewire the brain include a daily meditation practice, evoking sentiments of gratitude and positive social interactions.

9

Generosity and Happiness

You must have read about the Dead Sea in the Middle East. It receives fresh water from rivers, but it has no outlet. Since the water does not pour out, the sea is ten times more saline than the ocean. As a result, except for some bacteria and fungi, most other flora and fauna cannot survive in its waters. No wonder it is called the 'Dead' Sea.

Likewise, we have all been blessed with comforts to a smaller or greater extent. If we wish to thrive, we too must create an outlet for sharing our blessings with others. That outlet is generosity. Altruistic acts and giving are the best way to lead a flourishing life. The American movie *Pay It Forward* released in 2000 propagates this idea.

Nature has the attribute of giving built into her. Water quenches the thirst of others; trees give shelter and food. They inherently help others flourish.

Likewise, our higher self is conditioned to give to others. We simply need to tap into that quality and experience how fulfilling it is.

The *Subhashitas*, a literary genre of Sanskrit epigrammatic poetry, states:

> *pibanti nadyaḥ svayameva nāmbhaḥ*
> *svayaṁ na khādanti phalāni vṛkṣāḥ*
> *nādanti sasyaṁ khalu vārivāhāḥ*
> *paropakārāya satāṁ vibhūtayaḥ*　(verse 51.170)

'Just as the rivers do not drink their own water but flow for others' benefit, just as fruit-bearing trees do not eat their own fruit but bear it for others, and just as clouds do not drink their own rain but shower it down for others, so saintly devotees live simply for others.'

This chapter is dedicated to the beauty of giving and how it makes us happy.

Through Giving We Receive

Our abilities and wealth, and all that we have are gifts God has bestowed upon us. When we use them in the service of others, God blesses us with more talents and opportunities to serve. For example, when we uplift one that is emotionally hurt, we become mentally stronger ourselves and feel joy from within. Similarly, when we share wisdom with others, we also become wiser.

dān diye dhan na ghate, nadī ghate na nīr
apne hāth dekh lo, yoṅ kyā kahe kabīr

In this verse, Saint Kabir explains: 'As they flow towards the ocean, rivers keep giving from their waters, yet they do not dwindle. Philanthropists generously share their wealth, but do not become impoverished from it. Try it out for yourself and see the results. I am not saying this without a basis.'

The universal law of Nature is to always return manifold times what you give in service.

yadyadiṣhtatamam loke yatchati-priyamātmanaḥ
tataṅivedayenmahayāṁ tadānantyāya kalpate
(Shreemad Bhagavatam 11.11.41)

In this verse, the Supreme Lord states: 'Whatever is very dear to you, whatever you hold as immensely valuable, offer it in service to Me. I shall multiply it infinite times over and give it back to you.'

A wonderful way to experience joy is to start increasing the joy of others as the following story elucidates.

A Guru sent a message to his hundreds of disciples saying, 'Come to my ashram. I would like to share the secret of true happiness with you.' Upon their arrival, Guruji asked all to inflate a balloon and write their name on it. He then asked them to go and place their balloons in a nearby room.

All the disciples left their balloons in the room, as they had been told, and returned. Guruji then said, 'Now go back in again and find your own balloon!'

Pandemonium broke loose! There was utter confusion as people were tripping over each other in search of their individual balloons. Amidst the chaos, many balloons popped, increasing the disciples' dissatisfaction and strife.

Guruji called them back and said, 'Let me tell you a better way to do this. Pick any balloon, announce the name written on it, and hand it over to whom it belongs.'

The problem got resolved so easily. People were receiving their balloons from each other. With this new strategy, there was now peace. Guruji shared his words of wisdom, 'Therein lies the secret of happiness. When you hand over the others' happiness to them, you automatically receive it for yourself.'

Joy behaves very much like a balloon. If you only go searching for your own, it will most likely burst. But if you strive to give others joy, your happiness will also grow. This is the law of the Universe.

Helping Others Is What Makes Us Human

Helping others is the simplest expression of love. Assisting an elderly person cross the road or carrying someone's groceries to their home—these are small acts of compassion. Taking care of a loved one in sickness or helping an unlettered person fill out a form—again small acts of caregiving that go a long way.

Society has a mix of both, the strong and the vulnerable. We must do our part to assist those in need. After all, empathy and self-sacrifice are the values that make us human.

Several years ago, anthropologist Margaret Mead was asked what she considered to be the sign that an ancient society was civilized. Everyone expected her to talk about clay pots, grinding stones or fishing hooks.

However, Mead responded with an unanticipated answer. She said that the first sign of civilization in ancient societies was a femur (thigh bone) that had been broken and then healed. She elaborated further. In the animal kingdom, having a broken thigh bone is equivalent to death. You cannot run from danger. You cannot reach the river for a drink or even gather food. You are, therefore, meat for prowling beasts. No animal can survive from scavenging predators long enough for their broken leg to heal.

If, however, a broken femur had healed, it confirmed that someone had taken care of the injured. The wound was tied up, the person was carried to safety and tended until recovery. As a result, Mead concluded that helping someone else through difficulty is where civilization starts.

Whether it be towards our family or community, we must cultivate a compassionate heart. While the fittest are known to survive and thrive, it is important to ensure the same for the weak as well. Through kindness and service, we all can do our small bit for the vulnerable to make this world more beautiful. In the process, we too will achieve a happier state of mind.

Serving Others Removes Our Sorrows

Difficult situations can leave us feeling miserable and hopeless. Thinking of our own distress, we subject ourselves to depressing thoughts and behaviours. If, however, we shift our focus away from ourselves to the good we can do for others, we overcome self-sabotaging thoughts for ourselves as well. And in adding value to someone's life, we achieve a sense of accomplishment and purpose.

A young woman went to a happiness counsellor. Though she was wealthy and beautiful, she felt her life was hollow and unfulfilling. She had recently lost her husband. Since then, all her expensive attire, furniture and assets seemed worthless. These feelings had taken her into deep depression.

'The office cleaning lady, Premlata, seems to be a very happy person,' the happiness counsellor said to her. 'Let us find out the secret of her happiness.' He invited Premlata to the room and asked her how she had found her happiness.

Premlata explained, 'Two years ago, my husband died of cancer. One month later, my son was killed in a car accident. After them, I had no one left and nothing to live for. Thinking of the desolation that awaited me ahead put me in deep despair. I stopped smiling, couldn't sleep and even considered ending my life.

'Then one day, while I was returning home from the market with groceries, a little kitten followed me home. When I went in, the sweet little thing began meowing outside my door. My heart melted, and I placed milk in a saucer on my doorstep. The hungry kitten lapped it all up with glee. Then, it began purring and rubbing its back against my leg. I broke into a smile. It was the first time in months that I had smiled.

'This made me think that if helping a little kitten could give me joy, then doing something nice for others would make me happier. So, the next morning I baked a cake for my sick neighbour. From then on, I made it a point to do small things for others to make them happy.'

Premlata ended profoundly, 'Today, I sleep better than anyone I know. I have found bliss by giving it to others.'

When we help others solve their problems, we forget our own. It is a win-win for everyone. While others feel cared for, we realize how privileged we are to have the opportunity to serve. Loving thoughts flood our being, giving inner gratification. As a result, we benefit both emotionally and spiritually.

Generosity Is Not Restricted to the Rich

I often hear people say they will become charitable when they are more prosperous. This is a mistaken notion. If we do not make a habit of giving when we start earning, most likely we will not be charitable when we become wealthy either. **Giving does not happen from the top of our bank account but from the bottom of our heart.**

The life of Padma Shri awardee, Harekala Hajabba, is very inspiring in this regard.

Harekala Hajabba never had the privilege of formal school education due to abject poverty while growing up. He used to earn his livelihood of about 150 rupees a day by selling fruits in the city of Mangaluru, Karnataka.

One day, a foreign tourist asked him about the price of oranges. Harekala was embarrassed at not being able to comprehend English. An acute realization of the importance of education dawned upon him.

This propelled him to start saving money with the noble idea of starting a school in his impoverished village. Eventually, investing his entire life savings, he purchased one acre of land with a small building so the children of the village would never suffer the same fate as him. A gift of love, the school now educates 175 students with classes up to grade ten.

The opportunities to serve the needy are unlimited and not contingent on our wealth or assets. All we require is the will to do so, and the ideas will pour forth.

We feel as though we may lose out if we expend our resources—time, effort and money—on others. However, this is not the case. As the saying goes: 'No one has ever become poor by giving.' Cultivating an attitude of generosity engenders abundance.

Charity—Our Eternal Responsibility

A mother abandons her selfish joys to perform her duty towards her children. She does not lose by giving to them, rather, she fulfils her God-given dharma. Similarly, charity is our responsibility to God. All that exists belongs to Him. Lovingly serving Him with all we have received from Him is our duty. That is why charity and service are greatly emphasized in all sacred books. The *Bhavishya Puran* states:

dānamekaṁ kalau yuge

'In the age of Kali, giving in charity is the only means for purification.' Similarly, the Ramayan states:

pragaṭ chāri pad dharm ke kali mahuñ ek pradhān
jen ken bidhi dīnheṅ dān karai kalyān

'Dharma has four basic tenets. Amongst them, one is the most important in the present age of Kali—give in charity by whatever means possible.' Let us take inspiration from this Puranic story.

Once, the celestial gods, human beings and demons were keen on gaining knowledge from their father, Brahma, the creator of this universe. In preparation for receiving divine knowledge, they all first observed self-restraint and practised austerities. Then, they went to Brahma and put forth their earnest request for enlightenment.

Brahma said, 'Listen carefully, and I will guide you all.'

To the celestial gods, he said, 'Da'. Just one syllable.

To the human beings, he said 'Da'. Again, just one syllable.

To the demons, he said 'Da'. Same one syllable.

'Da, Da, Da,' was all the creator uttered. He then said, 'Now go and follow my instruction!'

Brahma mentioned the same syllable to all three, but it carried different meanings for each of them. The celestial gods are used to revelling in sensory pleasures.

They are addicted to endless enjoyment. So, 'Da' for them indicated dāmyata, *meaning 'restrain yourself and subdue your senses'.*

The demons are very cruel and have no qualms about inflicting harm upon others. Their nature is to demolish and destroy. Hence, to them, 'Da' indicated dayadhvam, *meaning, 'be compassionate to others, not cruel or hard-hearted'.*

Humans are inherently selfish and tend to accumulate and hoard beyond their needs. Hence, to them, 'Da' indicated datta, *meaning, 'give in charity'. We must not keep more than we need for our basic necessities for that is greed. Charity is the way to keep our greed in check.*

There are three stages in human life: 1) learn (acquire education and skills); 2) earn (use our talent to generate wealth); and 3) return (give back to the world). Most people focus on the first two but miss out the third. However, if we do not give back, our wealth will remain impure. Nature will then force us to spend on medical bills and doctors' fees. Therefore, to purify our wealth, we must open our hearts to charity.

Compare wealth to cow dung—both possess the potential to nurture. Cow dung is excellent manure, rich in nutrients for plants. When spread out on the earth, it improves the soil and nourishes vegetation. But if piled in one place, it breeds pathogens and stinks.

The nature of wealth is much the same. When hoarded in one place, it increases pride and breeds vices. But when distributed, it bestows prosperity and well-being. Money is an extension of ourselves. It can reach where we cannot—to feed the hungry, nurse the sick, clothe the poor and shelter the weak.

Money, however, is not the only means for charity. Service can take many forms. Volunteering your time, energy or skills can add as much or even more value than money. Small acts of kindness are a good way to get started. Think about a friend or a colleague who needs support. For those who are insecure, give them confidence. For those who desire a better tomorrow, show them hope. At the workplace, be generous in sharing your expertise. Make it a habit to praise or compliment others.

No matter how small they may be, acts of goodness always touch others' hearts. So, let us look upon giving as a privilege and an opportunity bestowed on us by God. With such understanding, giving becomes a lifestyle and habit.

How Much to Give?

The miserly do not spend anything on others and very little on themselves. However, it turns out that misers are the biggest givers. Why? Because upon death, they leave it all behind! That is why when a wealthy person dies, people do not ask, 'How much did the billionaire take with him?' Rather, they ask, 'How much did Sethji leave behind?' The factual answer is, 'Everything!' No one can take any material possessions to the afterlife.

Remembering this, put your money to good use. The *Skanda Puran* instructs:

nyāyopārjita vittasya daśhamānśhena dhīmatah
kartavyo viniyogaśhcha īśhvaraprityarthameva cha

'Whatever you earn by lawful means, consider it your duty to offer 10 per cent of it for the pleasure of God.' The scriptural recommendation of 10 per cent is the bare minimum that we must offer. However, we should try and exceed that. In fact, the Shreemad Bhagavatam states:

yāvad bhriyeta jaṭharaṁ tāvat svatvaṁ hi dehinām
adhikaṁ yo 'bhimanyeta sa steno daṇḍam-arhati   (7.14.8)

'One is entitled to keep only as much wealth as is necessary for one's maintenance (the rest must be given away in charity). If one accumulates more than one's need, one is a thief in the eyes of God and will be punished for it.'

Factually, **it is not the amount we give, but the spirit of service that pleases God.**

During British rule in India, Madan Mohan Malviya proposed the idea of a Hindu university in Banaras. He travelled throughout the country to gather donations.

Many kings and wealthy businessmen donated to the cause. As a token of appreciation, their names were included in the roll of honour.

One rickshaw puller offered twelve annas towards the cause. That was merely seventy-five paise. Malviya added his name to the honour roll as well. People questioned him as to why such a small amount deserved recognition alongside the large sums received. Malviya explained, 'The poor man offered his three days' earnings. His sacrifice was equally big, if not bigger, than the kings who donated thousands of rupees.'

When you donate for a noble cause, remember your Divine Father, who never gets tired of giving.

When to Give?

There is no time like the present to give. Money sitting idle often gets wasted on low-value activities. It is best utilized for a good cause. Many people wait for special occasions or festivals to donate, thinking they are auspicious times. However, for good work, all days are opportune.

A poor Brahmin once approached the great King Yudhishthir for financial help in getting his daughter married. Yudhishthir agreed to support him but was preoccupied with affairs of the kingdom, so he told the Brahmin to come the next day.

Yudhishthir's younger brother, Bhimsen, happened to hear this. He instructed everyone in the city of Hastinapur to begin festivities. When Yudhisthir inquired about the reason for the celebrations, Bhimsen responded, 'Brother, you have conquered death! That is why you asked the Brahmin to come tomorrow. You were so sure that you will be alive tomorrow.'

Yudhisthir understood his fallacy. He immediately summoned the Brahmin and gave him the donation.

Time does not stop for anyone. We must not procrastinate when engaging in good deeds. Later is always in the future, while the opportunity to give is in the here and now. It may or may not present itself again because there is no guarantee of our life. Therefore, the best time to give is the present.

Various Kinds of Charity

True charity is that which is done, not with a feeling of superiority, but with a sense of gratitude to God for the opportunity to be of service. There are gradations in it, from inferior to superior.

1. Tamasic Charity: The Bhagavad Gita states:

adeśha-kāle yad dānam apātrebhyaśh cha dīyate
asat-kritam avajñātaṁ tat tāmasam udāhritam

(verse 17.22)

Charity given to an undeserving person and at an inappropriate time is in the mode of ignorance. For example, money given to an alcoholic. He could use it to get a drink and then commit murder. Both the recipient and donor become liable for the offence committed.

2. **Rajasic Charity:** Again, the Bhagavad Gita guides us:

yat tu pratyupakārārtham phalam uddishya vā punaḥ
dīyate cha pariklishtam tad dānam rājasam smritam

(verse 17.21)

Donation with the primary motive of recognition in society is in the mode of passion. For example, donating to a temple so that your name gets inscribed on its wall as a donor.

3. **Sattvic Charity:** According to the Bhagavad Gita:

dātavyam iti yad dānam dīyate 'nupakāriṇe
deshe kāle cha pātre cha tad dānam sāttvikam smritam

(verse 17.20)

Wealth donated for good causes without any expectations to well-meaning recipients is in the mode of goodness. Examples include providing clothes and basic necessities for the poor or giving for the research of new medical treatments for the betterment of humankind, and so on.

4. *Nirguna* **Charity:** Material charity is commendable; however, its benefits are limited to the body. Nirguna charity is beyond the three modes of material nature. It is spiritual service done at the platform of the soul, for its upliftment.

The Guru is a divine personality beyond the three gunas (modes). He distributes divine knowledge that helps reunite the soul with God thereby ending its suffering from the root. Hence, assisting the Guru in his mission for the welfare of humankind is the highest charity one can engage in. It attracts God's grace, and one progresses towards spiritual perfection.

Service—The Ultimate Attitude Towards Life

Service must become our attitude towards life, the primary intention, through which we find meaning and purpose for living. It should be the driving force that motivates us every day and in all our activities. Let me share my own learning in this regard.

As a child, I was extremely fond of soccer. I played it strenuously every day, even though my bodily frame and muscular structure were under par. The consequence was that when I was in grade eight, the ligaments in my knees gave way and snapped.

Switching to a lighter sport in high school, I took up tennis. I played it all the way through college. Although I was reasonably good at tennis, I never made it to my college team. What was the reason that limited my progress?

My serve was weak. And that made all the difference because a strong service is vital to the game. Thus, I decided that in life I would not allow such a handicap. I would, instead, make service my motto.

Service to God is our constitutional position. The *Chaitanya Charitāmṛit* states:

jīvera svarūpa haya kṛiṣhṇera nitya-dāsa
(*Madhya Leela*, 20.108)

'The soul is by nature the servant of God.' There are three types of service one can do—financial, physical and mental. However, there is one level of service that is the highest—giving our soul to God. The Bhagavad Gita states:

brahmāgnāvapare yajñaṁ yajñenaivopajuhvati
(verse 4.25)

'They worship perfectly who offer the self as sacrifice in the fire of the Supreme Truth.'

Offering one's soul to God is called *atma samarpan* or *atmāhutī*. Yogi Shree Krishna Prem has described it beautifully: 'In this world of dust and din, whenever one makes *atmāhutī* in the flame of divine love, there is an explosion, which is grace, for no true *atmāhutī* can ever go in vain.' Consider this heart-touching example.

A little girl, Meera, was suffering from a rare and dangerous disease. Her only hope of recovery was a blood transfusion from her five-year-old brother, Sukrit. He had remarkably survived the same illness and had antibodies in his system to fight the disease.

The doctor approached Sukrit and explained how his blood could save his sister's life. Upon hearing the doctor's request, Sukrit's jaw fell in fear. But he gave his consent. He lay next to his sister in the hospital, and the blood transfusion began. Two full units of blood were removed from his body and transfused to his sister.

With a tremble in his voice, Sukrit asked, 'Doctor, when will I start to die?' Innocent and naïve, the little boy had assumed he was giving his life to save his sister's.

This is the attitude we want to adopt towards God. **Selfless giving of your soul to God is the highest expression of love and service. In doing so, you resign all selfish desires and submit to His wish alone. It is so powerful that it enslaves God Himself.**

You can read more about this in the last chapter, 'The Ultimate Happiness'. Before that however, we will look at what great thinkers, philosophers, spiritual teachers and writers had to say about happiness throughout history.

Summary

- God has bestowed many gifts upon us. When we use them in the service of others, God blesses us with more talents and opportunities to serve.

- Empathy and self-sacrifice are the values that make us human. We must do our part to assist those in need.

- When we help others solve their problems, we forget our own. It is a win-win for everyone.

- The opportunities to serve the needy are unlimited and not contingent on our wealth or assets.

- All that exists belongs to God. Lovingly serving Him with all we have received from Him is our duty and responsibility.

- The scriptures instruct us to offer 10 per cent of what we earn for the pleasure of God.

- We must strive to adopt a service attitude in life. There are three types of service one can do—financial, physical and mental.

- However, there is one level of love and service that is even higher—offering our soul itself to God.

10

Prominent Perspectives on Happiness through the Ages

Since the urge to be happy is hardwired into our soul, it is not surprising that throughout the ages, philosophers in the East and West had pondered deeply over it. They delved into the nature of happiness and the kinds of happiness available to humans. They discussed harmful and beneficial pleasures and suggested ways to lead a happy life. Some categorically rejected the idea that true happiness is available during our sojourn on the planet earth. Others were convinced that it awaits us in the afterlife.

Here, we will explore teachings of the most eminent of these thought leaders. Reading about their views is like travelling down history lane while watching sights from all the different continents. With an eye on brevity, we will primarily focus on their views about happiness.

Socrates (469–399 BC) lived in Athens, Greece. It was a time when Greece was engaged in the gruesome Peloponnesian War with Sparta, and the Greeks had a very pessimistic view of human existence. They believed that happiness was a rare occurrence, reserved only for those whom the Gods favoured. Socrates was the first eminent personality in the West who argued that happiness was achievable through human effort.

He taught that happiness does not depend on what we possess but on how those things are used. For example, wise people will use wealth intelligently, while foolish people will squander money unwisely, making their life even worse. Consequently, money is only a 'conditional good', felt Socrates. In contrast, happiness is an 'unconditional good', because it is the end goal of our activities, and everyone desires it.

Socrates taught that the way to achieve true happiness is by becoming virtuous. If we lead a life of justice and morality, we will develop the inner harmony to be happy even in the direst circumstances.

Aristotle (384–322 BC) was a student of Plato, who in turn, was a student of Socrates. His thoughts influenced Europe for a thousand years and are often called the 'Aristotelian years'. He enshrined happiness as the central purpose of human existence.

In his work, *Nicomachean Ethics,* he addressed the question: 'What is the goal of life?' He explained that we seek wealth, reputation and luxuries only because we believe they will make us happy. They are, thus, a means for achieving happiness. However, happiness is always an end in itself.

He was convinced that true happiness requires many ingredients, including physical health and material goods. However, the most important of these is a good moral character, which he called 'complete virtue'. Like the Buddha's middle path, Aristotle talked of maintaining a 'mean', which is a balance between sensual pleasures and harsh asceticism.

Mencius (372–289 BC) was a Chinese philosopher, widely accepted as the second 'Confucius'. He laid great emphasis on the role of the mind in the quest for happiness. He believed that humans are intrinsically good; they have a Tian-like nature because they are pieces of Tian, the Supreme Power. Everyone, therefore, has 'sprouts of virtue' in them. These are sentiments, such as sympathy, empathy and self-sacrifice.

Mencius opined that when our actions are not righteous, they do not provide us satisfaction. Then the sprouts of virtue shrivel up. Instead, our intrinsic divinity must be nourished through good thought and righteous action. This floods the body with vital energy, called *qi*, and one experiences joy and satisfaction. Mencius thus suggests the practice of virtue because it will make us happy.

Epicurus (341–270 BC) lived in Athens a little after Plato and Aristotle. He subscribed to the idea of empirical evidence, meaning 'that which can be experienced'. Since pleasure is immediately perceptible, he considered it the only valuable thing. He is famous for his theory of Hedonism.

Today, a lifestyle of wanton sensual gratification is labelled hedonistic. However, this connotation of the word would have shocked Epicurus, who taught it quite differently. He explained that a pleasurable life is lived by avoiding unnecessary desires and finding contentment in simple things. This leads to inner tranquillity.

Epicurus' example of a 'Pleasure Garden' was one where we engage in discussion on philosophy amidst the beauty of nature. In the background, a lyre plays, with the cool Mediterranean breeze blowing. In this garden of pleasure, we choose the fellowship of friends and family instead of physical indulgences, such as sex, intoxication and gluttony. Quite a contrast to the modern connotation of hedonism!

Zeno of Citium (334–262 BC) was the founder of Stoicism, a school of philosophy later made famous by Marcus Aurelius. Zeno taught that virtue is sufficient for happiness. Hence, it is unwise to pursue a life filled with lavish desires. These only poison us by giving way to more desires.

Zeno taught that we experience inner turmoil due to non-acceptance of negative circumstances. We cannot always change the circumstances, but we can change our thinking.

If we can learn to be indifferent to painful situations, we will grow in virtue and become a sage. The sage could be sick and yet happy, disgraced and yet happy, poor and yet happy. The Stoics, therefore, spend their time trying to cultivate dispassion.

St Augustine (354–430 AD) was a theologian and philosopher who lived in Hippo, Africa. He is viewed as one of the most important Church Fathers. His writings have greatly influenced the thought process of Western philosophy.

Augustine believed our fundamental problem is related to love—our love is misplaced. We either love the wrong things, or we love the right things in the wrong way. For example, fame, wealth and power are unworthy of our love. Likewise, we love people excessively. We give them the place in our heart that is reserved for God, and this undermines our happiness.

Instead, if we love God first, our love will be properly ordered. Then, we will still love all the good things in creation but in the right way and to the right extent. Doing so will enhance our experience of happiness in this life. But the biggest pleasure, said Augustine, is reserved for the heavenly afterlife. Anticipation of that can presently be the source of joy.

Abu Hamid al-Ghazali (1058–1111 AD) was an Islamic philosopher, prolific Sunni Muslim author and mystic. He emphasized happiness in his teachings and wrote the *Alchemy of Happiness*.

Al-Ghazali taught that happiness is not found in physical things; it requires the transformation of the self. Presently, our hearts are covered with dust by the passions of the body. We must know our true nature as spiritual beings. Then, we must cleanse our heart, just as we polish a mirror. The inner cleansing requires following moral discipline and eliminating selfish desires.

Al-Ghazali claimed that true happiness comes from union with the Divine. Only a few people have attained this state. These are the prophets who appear from time to time as messengers to remind human beings about the ultimate goal of their life.

Thomas Aquinas (1224–1274 AD) had a deep impact on Western philosophy and theology. The Roman Catholic Church called him the 'Angelic Doctor'. His goal was to integrate all knowledge with Christianity. In the more than forty books he wrote, he integrated Greek philosophy with the Christian faith.

His view on happiness lies midway between Aristotle and Augustine. Aristotle had believed that complete happiness is possible in this lifetime, while St Augustine had taught that true happiness is in the heavenly afterlife. Thomas Aquinas acquiesced that imperfect happiness (felicitas) is available to us on earth, but perfect happiness (beatitude) is available only in the spirit world. It comes through a mystical vision of God, which is not possible in the mortal body and is granted to the purified soul in the afterlife.

John Locke (1632–1704 AD) was an English philosopher whose ideas were instrumental in setting into motion the American and French revolutions. He coined the phrase 'pursuit of happiness' and said it is an essential aspect of liberty. The phrase was later adopted by Thomas Jefferson in the American Declaration of Independence. Key parts of the Constitution of the United States have also been lifted from Locke's political writings.

Locke emphasized the distinction between 'false pleasures' and 'true pleasures'. False pleasures, he said, provide immediate gratification that is followed by pain, regret and guilt. For example, narcotics bestow a momentary euphoria. But their long-term effects on the body and mind are damaging.

Animals are completely tied to their passions and do not have the freedom to rise above them. As humans, we possess the freedom to use our intellect to cut through the illusion of false pleasures. Our desire for true happiness enables us to reject the glass of wine in favour of higher and even higher pleasures. Therefore, said Locke, the pursuit of happiness is the foundation of morality and civilization.

Immanuel Kant (1724–1804 AD) was a German philosopher and one of the most influential figures in modern Western philosophy. However, his ideas on happiness were the reverse of Locke's. He believed happiness is a very indeterminate concept, impossible to attain. No matter how rich one becomes, the thought of becoming richer remains. It is the same with all other desires. Hence, it is a mistake to pursue happiness.

Kant taught that we should not make major life decisions based on the criteria that they will bring us happiness. Instead, we should pursue a life of morality and good action. Morality, felt Kant, has definitive answers. It is easy to know whether or not we have behaved morally.

Kant did believe that perfect happiness can be attained after death. This, he said, is the incentive provided by God for following morality. Else, there would be no rational answer to the question, 'Why bother being moral?'

Jeremy Bentham (1748–1832 AD) was a British philosopher regarded as the 'Founder of Utilitarianism'. He argued that the moral quality of our actions should be judged by their impact on our happiness. Thus, polite behaviour, liberty and bodily health are good because they promote happiness.

Bentham defined happiness as the sum of our pleasures reduced by the sum of pains. Public institutions, law and social policy should aim at maximizing happiness. Hence, decisions should be taken on the principle: 'greatest happiness for the greatest number of people'.

William James (1842–1910 AD) was born in New York. He went on to become the leading philosopher and psychologist of his time. He founded 'Pragmatism', a school of philosophy. It holds that any truth can only be validated by the practical effects of its beliefs.

James had many insights regarding happiness. The foremost of them was the idea that joy comes by aligning ourselves with a higher purpose. It does not matter whether the higher purpose has any rational basis or not.

James realized through his own battle with depression that humans possess free will. By exerting their freedom of choice, they can alter their psychological state. He believed that happiness is created and not discovered. Thus, he taught, 'Believe that life is worth living, and your very belief will help create the fact.'

Abraham Maslow (1908–1970 AD) is famous for his theory called 'Hierarchy of Needs'. He wanted to comprehend what humans are capable of and what motivates them to great heights. He concluded that there is a sequence of needs. Only after lower needs are met do people aspire for fulfilling higher needs.

The lowest in the hierarchy are physiological needs, such as food, water, sleep and sex. If these are not fulfilled, people become preoccupied with them above all else. After they are taken care of, as per Maslow, safety needs become a paramount concern. People focus on physical, economic, social and psychological safety. When these are met, one gets the confidence to face the adventure of life.

Third, claimed Maslow, come belongingness and love needs. As social beings, we humans wish to establish meaningful connections with people and be involved in communities. Fourth in the hierarchy are esteem needs. When these are satisfied, then one gains the psychological freedom to be creative and generous.

The fifth and final is the need for self-actualization. It is the yearning for self-growth—to become the best version of ourselves. As per Maslow, those who strive for self-actualization lead joyous lives, while others experience only flashes of happiness.

Martin Seligman (1942 AD–) is the pioneer of 'Positive Psychology', which is the scientific study of what makes people thrive and flourish. It aims to build the good life rather than repairing the bad. It examines how average people can become great, not merely how depressed people can be made normal.

Prior to Seligman, psychology had mainly focused on neuroses, abnormalities and traumas. When Seligman took over as the president of the American Psychological Association in 1998, he announced a new direction to the study of human emotions and behaviour.

As per Seligman, happiness has three dimensions—the Pleasant Life, the Good Life and the Meaningful Life. The Pleasant Life involves savouring basic pleasures, such as companionship and physical needs. The Good Life is achieved by nourishing our unique virtues and strengths for developing a flourishing personality. The Meaningful Life is the deep fulfilment we get by employing our strengths for a purpose greater than ourselves.

This completes our tour of philosophers and psychologists who made happiness the primary foundation of their philosophy. You may have wondered about the absence of Indian personalities from this list. Why is that so? Does that mean that Indian thought did not contribute to this topic? Quite the contrary. Indian sages, saints, seers, kings and philosophers all had profound views on happiness and ultimate happiness. It would take an entire book or more to cover those thoughts.

To keep it simple, in the next chapter, we will discuss only Vedic perspectives and the thinking of hundreds of eminent Indian rishis, sages, yogis and acharyas aligned with the Vedic viewpoint.

Also, note that as a mark of respect we have excluded mention of religious personalities of different faiths and will do the same for Indian saints too.

Summary

- Philosophers in the East and West pondered deeply on the nature of happiness and the kinds of happiness available to humans.

- Socrates was the first eminent personality in the West who argued that happiness was achievable through human effort. Aristotle was convinced that true happiness requires many ingredients. The most important of these is a good moral character, which he called 'complete virtue'.

- Mencius believed that our intrinsic divinity must be nourished through good thought and righteous action.

- Epicurus held the view that pleasure is immediately perceptible, and hence the only valuable thing. He is famous for his theory of Hedonism. Zeno of Citium was the founder of Stoicism. He felt that virtue is sufficient for happiness, while lavish desires only poison us.

- St Augustine believed our fundamental problem is related to love—our love is misplaced. He proposed we must love God first. Then, our love will be perfectly ordered.

- Abu Hamid al-Ghazali, an Islamic philosopher, claimed that true happiness comes from union with the Divine.

- Thomas Aquinas acquiesced that imperfect happiness (felicitas) is available to us on earth, but perfect happiness (beatitude) is available only in the spirit world.

- John Locke emphasized that the pursuit of happiness is the essential aspect of liberty and a free society.

- Immanuel Kant believed happiness is a very indeterminate concept, impossible to attain. Instead, we should pursue a life of morality and good action.

- Jeremy Bentham argued that the moral quality of our actions should be judged by their impact on our happiness, which is the sum of pleasures minus pains.

- William James propounded that joy comes by aligning ourselves with a higher purpose. He believed that happiness is created and not discovered.

- Abraham Maslow is famous for his 'Hierarchy of Needs' theory. He concluded that there is a sequence of needs. Only after lower needs are met do people aspire for fulfilling higher needs.

- Martin Seligman is the pioneer of positive psychology, which is the scientific study of what makes people thrive and flourish. It examines how average people can become great, not merely how depressed people can be made normal.

11

Vedic Perspective on Happiness

What is the Vedic perspective on happiness? The answer is not so simple. Before we dive into it, let us get an appreciation of the position of the Vedic scriptures in the Indian culture, and then we will take a look at their perspective on happiness. So, let us take a closer look at it.

Through the ages, Bharat, or India, has traditionally been looked upon by the rest of the world as the land of spirituality. Thousands of sages, from the Himalayas to Kanyakumari, blessed its sacred soils with the dust of their holy feet. Their life and teachings left an indelible impact on the beliefs and aspirations of the people. The Supreme Lord also took avatar in Bharat in various forms, such as Ram, Krishna, Kapil, Rishabh, Buddha, Dattatreya, and so on. The result was a culture where devotion to God thrived. Consequently, spiritual attainment was exalted in people's value systems as the foremost of virtues.

The Inward Orientation of the Indian Culture

History informs us that whenever a civilization grew powerful, it went out to plunder, conquer and enslave. In contrast, the Indian civilization turned its attention to inner conquests, even though at one time India accounted for a third of the world's GDP.

Shankaracharya nicely portrayed this inner quest in his *Prashnavali*, with the question: *jagad jitam kena* 'Who shall win over the world?' The answer he provided was: *mano hi yena* 'One who conquers the mind'.

The Western world is outwardly directed. External accomplishments are what people get stirred up about. The social narrative is also predominantly about material success. Power and prestige are the prized currencies of the majority. The reason for this value system can be traced back to 2500 years in the past.

The present Western civilization has its roots in Greece, from where it evolved to its present form via the Roman, Portuguese, Spanish, French and English civilizations. The ancient Greek culture laid the foundation for the Western world. Greece, in turn, was greatly influenced by its epics—the Iliad and the Odyssey. These two classics had mundane romance themes as their epicentres. Hence, the civilization they helped forge became a materialistically oriented one.

Likewise, the culture of India too was forged by its great epics—the Ramayan and the Mahabharat. These sacred works were steeped in devotion with the pastimes of God as their central theme. Consequently, Indian culture evolved as profoundly devotional.

The impact can be felt even today in most Indian art and dance forms, where cultural performances are customarily based upon themes from the Dasavatar, Ramayan, Mahabharat and the Puranas. Bhakti seems to run in the blood of the people, so much so that moksha, samadhi and God-realization are looked upon by the masses as the ultimate goal of human life.

What Is Culture?

Regarding culture, a question is pertinent here. In India too, we find large sections of materialistic people, atheists, non-believers and the like. Not every Indian is spiritually inclined. Then how can we call the country's culture a spiritual one?

To answer the question, let us first understand the term 'culture'. We all have personal views regarding what is excellence in thought, beliefs, actions and character. When a community of people develop common points of reference regarding excellence, and these get passed down from generation to generation, they become the culture of the community.

In the Indian civilization, these points of reference developed commonality on the superiority of spiritual pursuits. As a result, Indian society largely seems to agree that the highest accomplishment in life is spiritual perfection.

For this reason, in any congregation, if a saint is present, they are accorded the seat of honour. Whether it be a corporate boardroom or a political meeting, if a saint happens to grace it, they are given the pride of place.

In the last many decades, Western culture has had a strong influence on the Indian population. Multinational corporations and media houses such as Netflix, Hotstar and HBO have been hugely successful in selling their wares in the country. As a result, the proliferation of Western media has eroded Indian values, beliefs and customs. And yet, in the midst of a huge wave of materialism, spirituality continues to thrive in the mindsets of many.

Let us now talk a little bit about the scriptures that have nourished the Indian culture.

The Vedas—Basis of Indian Spirituality

Amongst the Hindus, the Vedas are revered as the highest of the holy books. They are not the creation of a human mind. They were manifest by God Himself in the heart of the first-born Brahma. From him, they were passed down from master to disciple by oral tradition. Hence, another name for them is *shruti*, which means 'knowledge received through the ear'.

These Vedas are the eternal knowledge of God, which He manifests again and again at the beginning of every cycle of creation. These sacred books, therefore, are also called *apauruṣheya*—not of human creation. And they are respected as the ultimate authority on spiritual matters:

> *bhūtaṁ bhavyaṁ bhaviṣhyaṁ cha sarvaṁ vedāt prasidhyati* (*Manu Smriti* 12.97)

'Any spiritual text must be validated by the knowledge of the Vedas.'

The Vedas have various sections amongst which the Upanishads are the most important. Since they are esoteric, the same knowledge of the Upanishads is explained more simply in the Puranas, Ramayan, Mahabharat, Smritis and other sacred texts. All these scriptures together form the body of knowledge called 'Vedic literature'.

These holy books present astonishingly clear concepts on the topic of happiness. Their logic and clarity fully satisfy the intellect, leaving no scope for doubt. Let us now dive deep into them for priceless gems of wisdom.

The Varieties of Happiness We Can Savour

As per the Vedic scriptures, joy is broadly of two kinds—material pleasures and spiritual bliss. We will discuss material pleasures first.

Material nature has three gunas (modes of functioning). The Bhagavad Gita states:

sattvaṁ rajas tama iti guṇāḥ prakṛiti-sambhavāḥ
nibadhnanti mahā-bāho dehe dehinam avyayam

(verse 14.5)

'O mighty-armed Arjun, the material energy consists of three gunas—sattva, rajas and tamas. These modes bind the eternal soul to the perishable body.'

In accordance with gunas, material pleasures fall in three categories. Let us briefly understand each of them.

Tamasic Happiness

In the Bhagavad Gita, Shree Krishna explained this to Arjun as:

yad agre chānubandhe cha sukhaṁ mohanam ātmanaḥ
nidrālasya-pramādotthaṁ tat tāmasam udāhṛitam

(verse 18.39)

Pleasure in the mode of ignorance is experienced through intoxicants, laziness, violence and gambling.

People habituated to savouring it become inclined to sloth and sleep. Social duties seem burdensome to them. Addicted to it, people do not even hesitate committing immoral behaviour for fulfilling their self-will.

Tamasic happiness, thus, increases the cover of darkness over the soul. It destroys the intellect's ability to distinguish right from wrong. Very often, the relief it provides is merely a benumbing of the intellect. 'My mind was troubling me too much; I was unable to handle it. So, I took a few pegs of whisky, and it helped me forget all my woes.' This is a graphic example of tamasic pleasure.

Rajasic Happiness

In verse 18.38 of the Bhagavad Gita, Shree Krishna continues:

viṣhayendriya-sanyogād yat tad agre 'mṛitopamam
pariṇāme viṣham iva tat sukhaṁ rājasaṁ smṛitam

This is fuelled by the lust for sensual enjoyment. Our senses desire their objects of pleasure. The eyes wish to see beautiful things, the tongue desires to taste delicious foods, the ears want to hear exciting sounds, the nostrils love to smell stimulating aromas and the skin wishes to touch pleasurable objects.

Fulfilling these desires does provide temporary delight but the purpose is not served. Once the cravings are satiated, the pleasure goes away. So, we again make the same desires to relive the experience of the delight. In this repeated process of savouring sense objects, our mind becomes attached to them.

Thus, rajasic happiness promotes attachment for worldly things. Under its influence, we get engrossed in materialistic pursuits of fame, power, wealth, family and home. For the sake of these, people undertake intense activity. Consequently, the soul gets bound in the trap of materialistic life.

Sattvic Happiness

Finally, in verse 18.37, Shree Krishna explains:

yat tad agre visham iva parināme 'mritopamam
tat sukham sāttvikam proktam ātma-buddhi-prasāda-jam

This is the happiness we experience in cultivating knowledge, developing virtues and engaging in acts of kindness. These higher pleasures do not work up a torturous thirst in the mind. Rather, they engender peace and contentment.

The Bhagavad Gita refers to the mode of goodness as *prakāshakam* meaning 'illuminating'. Shree Krishna also describes it as *anāmayam* meaning 'full of well-being'. In contrast to the previous two modes, it is serene and uplifting. It nurtures tranquillity of the mind.

Yet even sattvic happiness does not satisfy the soul. The kind of bliss our soul yearns for is divine—transcendental to the three gunas. Understand this through an example.

Three bandits attacked a traveller who was passing through a forest. 'Let us kill him and steal all his wealth,' said the first bandit. The second said, 'No, do not kill him. We will simply tie him up and take away his belongings.'

Following on the second bandit's suggestion, they bound the traveller in ropes, stole his wealth and went away. After a little while, the third bandit returned. He untied the traveller. Then he took him to the edge of the forest. He showed the traveller the way out, and said, 'If you follow this path, it will take you out of the forest. I cannot get out myself, but I have shown you the way.'

The first bandit was tamo guna (the mode of ignorance), which literally wants to kill the soul by plunging it into addiction, rage and laziness. The second bandit was rajo guna (the mode of passion), which inflames lust in humans and binds the soul through endless worldly desires. The third bandit was sattva guna (the mode of goodness), which eradicates vices, reduces material discomfort and puts the soul on the path of virtue.

The story highlights that even sattva guna is within the realm of material nature. We must transcend it to reach the true bliss our soul seeks.

The Nature of Divine Bliss

Our soul is divine, and hence the happiness it seeks is also divine. Divine bliss must possess three attributes: *sat, chit* and *anand.*

1. *Sat* means everlasting, or eternal.

2. *Chit* means ever fresh, sentient.

3. *Anand* means it must be of infinite extent.

These three attributes hold the key to the secret of happiness. Let us probe them further.

Divine bliss is everlasting.

Material happiness comes and goes. Let us say, you went for a weekend vacation and had great fun. But then, on Monday, you had to get back to your humdrum office routine. That makes you miserable and squeezes out all the happiness of the vacation.

Can such pleasures—that have a beginning and an end—fulfil us permanently? Absolutely not! This kind of short-lived happiness is experienced by alcoholics regularly. They get a 'high' from their drinks, but it soon vanishes and is followed by a 'hangover' the next morning.

In contrast to this, our soul seeks pleasure that once attained, will always remain. This is *sat* happiness.

Divine bliss is ever fresh.

Material pleasures keep reducing even while savouring them. You see a newly released movie, and it gives you a thrill. But if you see it again, the pleasure decreases. View it a fourth time, and it feels torturous. It is the same movie, but the joy you get from it keeps diminishing.

However, our soul seeks a kind of bliss that will remain ever fresh. This is *chit* happiness.

Divine bliss is of infinite extent.

Happiness from material things is finite. Let us say someone becomes a senior manager in a multinational company and feels happy. But when she sees the Chief Operations Officer (COO), she thinks, 'O my God, look at him! I am only a senior manager while he is the COO.'

The example illustrates that if we perceive someone getting more pleasure than us, we become unhappy. Our soul is averse to being gratified with finite happiness and seeks *anand* or infinite bliss.

In conclusion, we want joy that is *sat-chit-anand* (permanent, ever fresh and infinite). Since material pleasures do not fulfil these parameters, the thirst of our soul remains unquenched. We must now seek divine bliss.

Where Is Infinite Bliss?

In the last section, we concluded that the bliss we hanker for is eternal, ever fresh and infinite. The question before us now is: Where can we find such divine bliss?

To know the answer, let us understand the nature of God. The *Taittirīya Upanishad* of the *Krishna Yajur Veda* narrates a story that throws light on it.

Sage Bhrigu was a prominent saint in Vedic history. When he desired to have a Guru, he thought, 'Why search any further? My father, *Varun devatā*, is such a big brahma jnani. Let me make him my Guru.'

Bhrigu then went up to *Varun devatā* and said: *adhīhi bhagavo brahmeti* 'Father! I have come today, not as your son but as a disciple. Who is that Supreme Power, Whom people call by many names, such as Brahman, Paramatma and Bhagavan?'

Varun responded: *yato vā emāni bhutāni jāyante, yen jātāni jīvanti, yatprayantyabhi-saṁviśhaṁti* 'God is He from whom the whole world has emanated; God is He within whom it is situated and God is He into whom creation will finally merge.'

Bhrigu could not comprehend such a profound statement. So, Varun asked him to perform austerities: *tapasa brahma vijijñāsasva tapo brahmeti.*

Bhrigu obeyed and engaged in severe austerities. By divine grace, his mind was purified, and he attained realization of the Truth. He then concluded: *ānando brahmeti vyajānāt, ānandādhyeva khalvimāni bhutani jāyante, ānanden jātāni jīvanti, ānandaṁ prayantyabhi-saṁviśhaṅtīti* 'Bliss is the nature of God! From Bliss, we all have emanated. In Bliss, we all are situated. And into Bliss we all shall merge one day.' On hearing Bhrigu's conclusion, Varun congratulated him for comprehending the nature of the Supreme.

The story emphasizes that God is divine bliss Himself. The *Chhāndogya Upanishad* states:

ānanda evadhastāt ānanda uparishṭāt
ānandaḥ purastāt ānandaḥ pakshchāt
ānanda uttarataḥ ānando dakshintaḥ
ānanda evedam 'sarvam

'The Supreme has Bliss below, Bliss above, Bliss behind, Bliss in front, Bliss to the left, Bliss to the right, Bliss inside, Bliss on the outside. Everything about Him is Blissful.'

The Vedic scriptures repeatedly refer to God as *sat-chit-anand,* meaning eternal bliss that is ever fresh and infinite. Here are a few such verses:

satyaṁ jñānam-anantaṁ brahma
                    (*Taittirīya Upanishad* 2.1.2)
satyaṁ vijñānam ānandaṁ brahma
                    (*Bṛihadāraṇyak Upanishad* 3.9.28)
ānandamayo'bhyāsāt (*Brahma Sutra* 1.1.12)
ānanda mātra kara pāda mukhodarādī (*Padma Puran*)

satya jñānāntānanda mātraika rasa mūrtayaḥ

(Bhagavatam 10.13.54)

All the above Vedic verses proclaim that the Supreme Lord is eternal, ever fresh and infinite bliss.

With this clarity regarding the connection between divine bliss and God, we are now in a position to understand the answer to an important question.

Why Do We All Want Happiness?

In the entire world, this question is satisfactorily addressed only in the Vedic scriptures. They declare that every part is naturally attracted towards its source. For example, a lump of mud is a part of the earth and is drawn towards it. If you throw the piece of mud up, it will automatically fall down, pulled by the gravitational force of the earth.

We all have heard of this story. Isaac Newton was sitting under an apple tree when the fruit fell on his head. Now, apples always fall on the ground. But Newton was the first to think, 'Why did the apple fall down; why did it not go up?'

This line of thinking led him to realize that the earth was pulling its little part, the apple, towards itself. He laid down his discovery as the Law of Gravitation.

In the same way, God is pulling His little parts to Himself. Since He is an Ocean of Bliss, we souls are fragments of divine bliss. The pull from the Lord is what we experience as the yearning for happiness.

This leads to the next question: Why have we not yet attained the divine bliss we seek?

The Mistake We All Made

Although we all are tiny fragments of the Supreme, we have our backs towards Him. This is called *vimukhata* (consciousness turned the other way). For this reason, God's illusory energy, maya, has overpowered us. Under its sway, we are covered by ignorance, as the following story illustrates.

A bottle of whisky was placed on a table. Three mice were playing on the floor underneath. A cat climbed atop the table and knocked the bottle over. It smashed on to the floor and created a puddle of the intoxicant.

The mice drank the whisky and became intoxicated. Now, the first mouse said, 'I am a king.'

The second mouse announced, 'I am the emperor of the world.'

'You both become whatever you wish,' said the third mouse. 'For my snack today, I am going to eat the cat.'

The whisky had destroyed the mice's intellect. Likewise, in the *mayadhīn* (materially bound) state, our intellect has suffered a reversal. The scriptures call this *viparyaya* (inverted knowledge). With the intellect in inversion, we commit three major mistakes: 1) We look on the temporary things of the world as permanent. 2) We mistakenly search for happiness in things that are actually sources of misery. Even more serious is our biggest mistake: 3) We see the material body—made of blood, stool, urine and mucus—as the self. We forget that we are divine souls, similar in quality to God Himself. This fundamental error sets us off on a wild goose chase.

The Compounding Mistake

If we begin our computation from the premise: 2 + 2 = 5, what will happen? All subsequent equations derived from it will be erroneous. Even further, with every computation, the mistake will keep proliferating. This is called a compounding mistake.

Likewise, our body is made from earth, water, fire, air and sky; it is a part of the world. The soul, in contrast, is divine; it is a part of God. However, the mistake we make is to forget our soul-nature. We identify with the body. Hence, our goal becomes attaining the pleasures of the body: 'What should I see to get happiness? What should I taste to feel blissful? What should I touch to get pleasure?'

In the bodily conception of the self, we chase the delights of the material senses, offering them to the divine soul. The problem is that no matter what we do, the soul within says, 'This is not my happiness. Give me infinite bliss.'

How the Mistake Can Be Corrected

We are presently looking for happiness in the wrong direction. Though we are divine beings, we are running after material happiness.

Suppose you take a fish out of the water and try to make it happy. You arrange for it to receive cool breezes from an AC unit. Massage it with perfumed oil. And feed it with its favoured food.

Do you think the fish will enjoy the luxuries? The poor creature cannot speak, but if it could, it would probably say, 'I want none of these. If you wish to make me happy, put me back into the water.'

Likewise, our real self—the divine soul—informs us, 'Material happiness does not satiate me. Give me infinite bliss that is eternal and ever fresh. Until then, I will remain thirsty.'

How will we get divine bliss? Simple. By correcting the mistake of identifying our 'self' as the body. When we decide we are divine souls, we will begin looking for divine happiness.

The point to note is that chasing happiness is not wrong. Even great saints, such as Soordas, Tulsidas, Meerabai, Nanak, Tukaram, Narsi, Ekanath, Namdev and Kabir, were trying to be joyful. But they were looking for it in the proper place. They were running towards the infinite Ocean of Bliss. In contrast, our quest for pleasure is like churning lime water and hoping for butter. Butter resides not in lime water but in yogurt.

The search for happiness, through the chapters of this book, has now brought us to God. In the next and last chapter, we will explore the varieties of spiritual bliss that exist in the realm of God.

Summary

- Amongst the Hindus, the Vedas are revered as the highest of the holy books. These Vedas are the eternal knowledge of God.

- The Vedic scriptures have nourished the Indian culture, making it profoundly devotional.

- As per the Vedic scriptures, we can savour varieties of happiness—tamasic (in the mode of ignorance), rajasic (in the mode of passion) and sattvic (in the mode of goodness). However, none of these satisfy the soul.

- Our soul is divine, and hence the happiness it seeks is also divine. This happiness must possess three attributes: *sat* (everlasting), *chit* (ever fresh) and *anand* (infinite in extent).

- Where can we find such divine bliss? The Vedic scriptures proclaim that God Himself is the Ocean of Bliss.

- Since we souls are His little parts, we naturally love our source, God, who is full of eternal, ever fresh and infinite bliss.

- The mistake we made was that we forgot our soul-nature and identified ourselves with the body.

- In the bodily conception of the self, we are chasing the delights of the material senses and offering them to our soul. But material happiness can never perfectly satisfy our soul.

- The divine happiness we seek is none other than God Himself.

12

The Ultimate Happiness

Our road to happiness has now reached the Ocean of Bliss. We have understood that the perfect joy the soul seeks is in God. And yet, the discussion is incomplete. Even in the personality of God, there are varieties of bliss that you can choose from. The highest amongst them should be our goal.

An ocean seems like one body of water from afar. But when you inspect it closely, you realize it is not a single undivided entity. Within it are varieties of aquatic creatures, coral, minerals, microbes and chemicals.

Similarly, based on the nature of their spiritual practice, devotees experience the bliss of God in several ways. In this last chapter of the book, we will look at the various kinds of divine bliss in the spiritual realm.

Brahmanand versus Premanand

Many people choose to worship the Supreme in His formless aspect, as the all-pervading Brahman. Others prefer to connect with Him in His personal forms, such as Ram, Krishna, Shankar and Durga. The bliss of the formless is called *Brahmanand*, while that of His personal form is called *Premanand*. Both are infinitely sweet. And yet, there is a distinction between them that needs to be understood.

Consider the following example:

Hiral had been married for fifteen years but did not have a child. Every time Hiral saw mothers with children, she lamented, 'If only I had a child, how exciting would it be.'

One day, Hiral realized she had a baby in her womb. She was thrilled, thinking, 'I am going to become a mother now.' For the next nine months, she experienced the travails of pregnancy but bore them joyfully. Finally, the day arrived when the child was born. Hiral began rearing her little one with utmost love.

If we ask Hiral now, 'Is the joy from your baby the same as when it was in the womb?'

Hiral will naturally respond, 'What are you saying? During pregnancy, I had just a feeling of the baby, but

I could not see my little one. Now, I can hug and serve my baby and witness his frolicking activities. This is true bliss.'

Similarly, if we worship the formless aspect of God, we will simply get a feeling of Him in the mind. We will be deprived of the bliss of having His darshan (divine vision). But if we worship His personal form, we will get to relish the sweetness of His Names, Forms, Qualities, Pastimes, Abodes and Associates. Hence, *Premanand*, or divine love bliss, is innumerable times sweeter than *Brahmanand*, the bliss of the formless Brahman. This does not in any way imply that *Brahmanand* is a material happiness. It is also the bliss of God, and hence, infinite, ever fresh and eternal. Yet, *Premanand* is even sweeter. Comprehend this through some worldly examples.

A rose is such a tender and beautiful flower. People wear it on their coat and appreciate its fragrance. But have you ever seen anyone wearing the thorny stem of a rose plant on their coat? Definitely not! Why? Because if they did, others would call them a fool. Why is there such a difference in perception between the stem and the flower? Even though parts of the same rose plant, the flower is immensely more fragrant than the stem.

Now consider a sandalwood tree. Its trunk itself is so full of fragrance. Imagine, if it had flowers, how fragrant would they be! And yet, the trunk and the flower would be parts of the same sandalwood tree.

Likewise is the distinction between the formless Brahman and the personal Form. They are both aspects of the same Supreme Divine Entity. Even so, the bliss of the personal Form, *Premanand*, is immensely sweeter than the bliss of the formless Brahman, *Brahmanand*.

However, many spiritual practitioners hold the reverse view. They opine that the attainment of the formless Brahman is the ultimate realization. Hence, they view devotion to the personal Form as an intermediate practice, and that in the end one must gravitate to the formless Brahman.

To refute this popular notion, we will visit some examples from history. These are real-life stories of saints who had attained Brahman realization. Yet, on connecting with the personal Form, they were instantly and naturally drawn towards it.

The Four Kumars Visit Vaikunth

The senior-most personalities in our universe, as per the Puranas, are the four Kumars—Sanat, Sanatan, Sanak and Sanandan. Brahma manifested them from his mind at the beginning of creation. He gave them the task of begetting further progeny. These Kumars, however, retained their childhood form and refused to grow any further. They were purified souls with no attachments or worldly desires. They felt if they became adults, maya would overpower them.

One day, they visited *Vaikunth*, the divine abode of Lord Vishnu. What happened to the Kumars on reaching *Vaikunth* is described in the Shreemad Bhagavatam.

tasyāravinda-nayanasya padāravinda-
    kiñjalka-miśhra-tulasī-makaranda-vāyuḥ
antar-gataḥ sva-vivareṇa chakāra teṣhāṁ
    saṅkṣhobham akṣhara-juṣhām api chitta-tanvoḥ

(verse 3.15.43)

The aroma of tulsi leaves from the lotus feet of the Supreme Divine Personality was carried by the breeze to the nostrils of the Kumars. It thrilled them with such joy that their absorption in *Brahmanand* ended. They were naturally drawn towards the *Premanand* of the personal form of God and lost interest in worshipping the formless Brahman. Imbued with devotion, they begged Bhagavan Vishnu for a boon: 'O Lord! May our mind be like a bee, drinking the nectar of Your lotus feet. For that, even if we have to go to hell, we do not mind. However, now we no longer wish to meditate on light.'

If *Brahmanand* is the highest bliss of God, then why would the four Kumars leave it to pursue *Premanand*?

Obviously, they found an even sweeter joy in the personality of God. A similar experience can be seen in the life of King Janak.

The Inspiring Story of King Janak

Mother Sita is worshipped in the Hindu tradition as the Mother of the universe. When She descended on the earth planet, King Janak had the honour of being Her father. He is also famous in history as 'Videha', which means 'one who has no perception of his body'. Janak was in such elevated consciousness that with one hand in the fire and another hand on his queen, he could still keep his mind absorbed in Brahman.

He was also a worshipper of the formless Brahman. In fact, he would consider all names and forms in the world as *mithyā* (illusory and unreal). One day, he received the news that the great Sage Vishwamitra, accompanied by Ram and Lakshman, had come to Janakpur. Janak went to welcome them, but on seeing the divine form of Shree Ram, he was spontaneously immersed in loving devotion. The *Ramcharitmanas* describes:

> *mūrati madhur manohar dekhi,*
> > *bhayau bidehu bidehu biseṣhi*   (1.214.4)
> *sahaj birāgrūp manu morā,*
> > *thakit hota jimi chand chakorā*   (1.215.2)

brahm jo nigam neti kahi gāvā,
  ubhay beṣh dhari kī soī āvā   (1.215.1)

'On seeing the divine form of Lord Ram, Videha (Janak) became even more *videha* (lost further consciousness of his body). His mind was already detached from the world. Yet he observed that he had become attached to Ram on first sight. The affinity was as natural as the *chakor* bird feels for the moon. This made Janak wonder, "I have been worshipping the attributeless Brahman. Am I seeing the same Brahman today in His personal form as Ram?"'

The episode reveals the unsurpassable sweetness of *Premanand* in comparison to *Brahmanand*. Absorbed in divine love for Ram, Janak's mind naturally detached itself from the bliss of the formless Brahman.

Let us now read about Shukadev, the son of Ved Vyas.

Shukadev Paramhans—the Highest Amongst Mystics

Shukadev is looked upon with great reverence in Indian scriptures. He was such an elevated yogi that when he came into his mother's womb, he allowed his body to grow for nine months like any ordinary child. But then, he halted this growth and continued to remain in the womb for another twelve years.

Once, while his father, Ved Vyas, was reciting Vedic mantras, Shukadev spoke up, 'Father, you made a mistake in the enunciation.'

Ved Vyas was astonished at the unborn child's competence. He asked, 'Why do you not come out from your mother's womb?'

Shukadev responded, 'If I enter the world of maya, I will come under its spell. Here, I am protected.'

Devarshi Narad had to be called for help. He told the unborn baby that nothing would happen, and he should emerge. That was when Shukadev was born. He then immediately expanded his body to that of a twelve-year-old. In his state of utmost detachment from worldly things, he did not even seek permission from his father for sanyas, instead, he simply walked off.

Shukadev entered the forest and sat down in samadhi. Very quickly, he reached the seventh *bhoomika* (highest state of *nirvikalpa samadhi*).

A few years went by. One day, Ved Vyas's disciples discovered Shukadev in a deep trance. They tried jerking him to conscious awareness in many ways, but nothing worked. So, they went and related the matter to their Guru. Ved Vyas then taught them a verse from the Shreemad Bhagavatam describing the splendid beauty of Shree Krishna. On his instructions, the students went and related the verse in Shukadev's ear.

barhāpīḍaṁ naṭa-vara-vapuḥ karṇayoḥ karṇikāraṁ
bibhrad vāsaḥ kanaka-kapiśaṁ vaijayantīṁ cha mālām
randhrān veṇor adhara-sudhayāpūrayan gopa-vṛindair
vṛindāraṇyaṁ sva-pada-ramaṇaṁ prāviśhad gīta-kīrtiḥ
(10.21.5)

This verse describes the transcendental beauty of Shree Krishna. After grazing the cows in the forest during the day, He is now returning home in the evening. His head is adorned with a peacock crown. A *vaijayantī* garland is flowing down His chest. His upper body is draped with a yellow cloth, and as He walks, He is beautifying the earth with the marks of His lotus-like feet. On His lips is a flute, on which He is playing an enchanting melody, calling the *gopis* to Him.

Until he heard the verse, Shukadev had been meditating on divine light. On hearing the verse, the light turned into Shree Krishna. It thrilled every pore of Shukadev's body, and he pondered, 'Why was I running after the formless, when Shree Krishna is so blissfully enchanting?'

Shukadev came out of his samadhi, went back to Ved Vyas and heard the entire Shreemad Bhagavatam from him. That was the scripture he related to Maharaj Parikshit on the banks of the Ganga. Thus, the highest of mystics, Shukadev Paramhans, illustrated by his own life experience that the *Premanand* of the personal form is even beyond *Brahmanand*.

Finally, we will visit Uddhav, disciple of Guru of the *devatās*, Brihaspati.

Uddhav—Foremost of the Jnanis—Encounters the *Gopis*

When the Supreme Lord, Shree Krishna, descended on the planet about 5000 years ago, He brought with Him a treasure chest of divine love. However, His dear friend in Mathura, Uddhav, was a worshipper of the formless. That made Shree Krishna think, 'What will people say in future? They will question Me, "Why should we worship the personal form of God, when Your own friend worshipped the formless?"'

To correct the anomaly and reveal the glories of divine love, Shree Krishna sent Uddhav, the foremost of the jnanis, to meet the *gopis*, the foremost amongst the devotees. The encounter between the highest mystic on the path of jnana and the supreme devotees on the path of bhakti revealed the differences between these two spiritual paths.

The *gopis* viewed Shree Krishna as their Soul-Beloved and were deeply absorbed in devotion to Him. They could not forget Him even for a moment. However, after showering them with His love in Vrindavan, Shree Krishna left for Mathura. Separation from Him had created such intense longing for the Lord in the *gopis* that they felt their life-airs would leave their body at any moment.

Uddhav went to Vrindavan with the intention of giving them knowledge. His message was, 'You should not yearn for God. You are yourselves the Supreme Entity. Meditate on these four *mahavakyās* of the jnanis:

> *tatvamasi* (*Chhāndogya Upanishad* 6.8.7)
> *aham brahmāsmī* (*Brihadāraṇyak Upanishad* 1.4.10)
> *ayam-ātmā brahma* (*Māndukya Upanishad* mantra 2)
> *prajñānam brahma* (*Aitareya Upanishad* 3.3)

Consequently, you will realize there is only one entity in existence, which is Brahman. Then your experience of the world will become *sarvam khalvidam brahma* "Everywhere is Brahman".'

The *gopis* patiently listened to Uddhav's dissertation of jnana yog. When he finished, they revealed their own elevated state of Brahman realization. They said to him, in the words of a popular devotional song sung in Braj:

> *shyam tan shyām man shyām hi humāro dhan,*
> *ūdho hume āṭho yām shyām hi soṅ kām hai*

'Shyam (the Supreme Divine Personality, Shree Krishna) is our body; Shyam is our mind; Shyam is our wealth. O Uddhav, twenty-four hours a day, Shyam is the sole object of our works.'

śhyām hiye śhyām jiye śhyām bina nahiṅ jiye,
aṅdhe kī sī lākarī ādhār śhyām nām hai

'Shyam is in our hearts; Shyam is the basis of our life. Without Shyam, we cannot even live. Shyam's name is our support just like the cane to a blind man.'

śhyām jñān śhyām dhyān śhyām hī humāro prāṇ,
śhyām śhyām raṭat sakal braj dhām hai

'Shyam is our knowledge; Shyam is our meditation; Shyam is our very life-airs. The whole of this land of Braj keeps reciting Shyam's names from morning to night.'

ūdho tum bhaye baure pātī lai āye daure,
yog kahāṅ rākheṅ yahāṅ rom rom śhyām hai

'O Uddhav, are you crazy? What message of ashtang yog have you brought for us? We have no place for it as every pore of our body is full of Shyam.'

Uddhav was astonished at the elevated state of the *gopis*. He thought, 'I was only talking about *advait* (non-duality). In reality, however, I was in *dwait* (duality), for I saw others as separate from me and gave lectures. But look at these *gopis*! They are truly in non-duality; they are perceiving Shree Krishna everywhere, through all their senses and at all times.'

By the grace of the *gopis*, Uddhav became immersed in bhakti. When he returned to Mathura, he asked the Supreme Lord for a boon:

> *āsām-aho charaṇa-reṇu-jushām-aham syām*
> *vrindāvane kim-api gulma-lataushadhīnām*
> *yā dustyajaṁ sva-janam-ārya-pathaṁ cha hitvā*
> *bhejur-mukunda-padavīṁ śhrutibhir-vimrigyām*

(Bhagavatam 10.47.61)

'O Shree Krishna, these *gopis* have attained the state that even the greatest mystics have not. They have even renounced their family ties and comforts for Your sake. I yearn to become eligible for their grace. To receive their foot dust, I will consider it my greatest good fortune to be born in my next life as a creeper, a bush or a tree in Vrindavan.'

In this way, the highest of jnanis became detached from *Brahmanand* on experiencing an even higher form of bliss. Do note here that Uddhav did not long for *Premanand*. Rather, he longed for the foot dust of the devotees who were absorbed in *Premanand*.

Let us reiterate here that God is one, and hence His formless aspect and personal Form are both dimensions of the One. When that is the case, then what explains the distinction between *Brahmanand* and *Premanand*? For this, we will need to understand the three ways in which the one Supreme Divine Entity manifests in the world.

The Three Manifestations of God

We can realize God in three levels of proximity. Consider the following example.

If you see an aeroplane from afar at night, it appears as a light. When it comes closer, you perceive a shimmering form. And when you see it after it has landed, you realize, 'Oh! It is an aeroplane. I can see the cockpit, the windows and even some people inside.'

The same aeroplane seemed like light from far. As it came closer, it appeared to have a gleaming form. When it was right in front, you could clearly observe its details.

Likewise, God's personality is equipped with infinite energies, each unlimited in extent. He is complete with divine Names, Forms, Pastimes, Virtues, Associates and Abodes. But He can be realized at different levels of closeness, such as Brahman, Paramatma and Bhagavan. Sage Ved Vyas writes:

vadanti tatatva-vidastvaṁ jñanaṁ-advayaṁ
brahmeti parmātmeti bhagavāniti śhabdayate

(Bhagavatam 1.2.11)

'The One undivided Supreme manifests in this world in three ways: Brahman, Paramatma and Bhagavan. This has been stated by the knowers of the Truth.'

These are not three different Gods. They are three manifestations of the same one God, and yet, they differ in qualities. Just as water, steam and ice are the same substance, but their physical qualities are different.

Let us discuss them one at a time.

Brahman

It is the aspect of God which is everywhere in creation. In this omnipresent manifestation, God does not reveal His Forms, Virtues, and Pastimes. He merely exists, with eternality, knowledge and bliss.

The Vedas say:

eko devaḥ sarvabhūteṣhu gūḍhaḥ sarvavyāpī
(Śhwetāśhvatar Upanishad 6.11)

'There is only one God. He is seated in everything and in everyone.'

The realization of the all-pervading formless Brahman is a distant realization of God as a formless light. It can be compared to the aeroplane from far, which appeared to be like light.

Paramatma

This is the aspect of God that is situated in everyone's hearts. Seated within, He notes all our thoughts and actions, keeps account of them and gives the results at the appropriate time. We may forget what we have done, but He does not. If you were asked, 'What were you thinking twenty-five hours and fifteen minutes ago?', you would probably say, 'I do not remember.' However, God remembers all our thoughts at every moment of our life.

And not only for this life! Through endless lifetimes, wherever we went, God accompanied us. In past lives, when we were in a cow's body, God was there with us. When we were in a bird's body, God was again there with us. He is such a Friend of ours, who never leaves us, even for a moment.

The Bhagavad Gita states:

aham ātmā guḍākeśha sarva-bhūtāśhaya-sthitaḥ

(verse 10.20)

'O Arjun, I am seated in the heart of all living entities.'

Paramatma, the manifestation of God that is seated in everyone's hearts, is a closer realization, just as the plane was seen as a shimmering light form when it came closer. As the Paramatma, He possesses a Form and Virtues, but does not display any Pastimes.

Bhagavan

This is the aspect of God that descends in the personal form as an Avatar and also resides eternally in His divine abodes. It is the closest realization of the Supreme, just as the details of the plane become visible when it is in front of the observer.

The Shreemad Bhagavatam states:

krishnam-enam-avehi tvam-ātmānam-akhilātmanām
jagad-dhitāya so 'py atra dehīvābhāti māyayā

(verse 10.14.55)

'The Supreme Lord who is the Soul of all souls, descended in His personal form, as Shree Krishna, for the welfare of the world.'

The personal form is called Bhagavan. In it, He reveals all the sweetness of His Names, Forms, Virtues, Abodes, Pastimes and Associates. These exist in the Brahman and Paramatma as well, but They do not manifest. Just as a matchstick has fire in it, but it is latent. The fire manifests when it is struck against the igniting strip of the matchbox. Similarly, as Bhagavan, all the powers and aspects of God's personality which are latent in the other forms, are revealed.

Why God Becomes a Servant of His Devotees

We began the journey through the pages of this book in pursuit of happiness. Now we come to the final lap in the journey: **To experience the highest bliss, sacrifice your desire for happiness.**

As we progress on the path of bhakti, at one stage even the desire for happiness needs to be rejected. It is replaced with a yearning for the happiness of God. Then the goal of life becomes service for the pleasure of the Lord. Sage Narad states in his *Bhakti Darshan*: *tat sukh sukhitvam* 'The *gopis* did not want their own happiness. Instead, they rejoiced in their Supreme Beloved's happiness.'

Divine love is all about giving, without considering, 'What did I get in return?' In this regard, let us understand three principles—love, lust and business.

1) Love. This is affection for the beloved with the sentiment, 'What can I give?' The emotion here is give . . . give . . . give.

2) Lust. It is the reverse of love. 'What am I getting in this relationship?' Lust is filled with thoughts of take . . . take . . . take.

3) Business. In it, we do give but also keep an eye on what we are getting. The exchange here is: give-and-take, give-and-take.

From the above comparison, we can see that love is devoid of self-seeking. Loving devotees have only one desire, 'How can I make my Lord happy?'

Now, God is not a miser. When we strive for His happiness, He reciprocates by giving us the highest fulfilment. In fact, the bliss that God bestows on selfless devotees is even higher than His own.

The happiness that God experiences from His own personality is called *swarūpānand*, while the happiness that God bestows upon the soul when it engages in selfless devotion is called *swarūp shaktyānand*. Interestingly, *swarūp shaktyānand* is even sweeter than *swarūpānand*.

This means that God makes His devotees experience a joy sweeter than His personal joy. Then, the Lord sits within His devotees and relishes the same joy Himself. Thus, the bliss God gets from devotees is higher than His personal bliss. As a result, He becomes enslaved by the love of His devotees. The Ramayan states:

> *byāpak braham niranjan, nirgun bigat binod*
> *so aj prem bhagati bas, kausalya ken god*

'Bhagavan is without form or attributes and is all-pervading. And yet, under the sway of mother Kaushalya's love, He is sitting in her lap as Baby Ram.'

If we wish, therefore, for the ultimate fulfilment possible for the soul, then we must learn to love God selflessly. In such devotion, only one desire remains—service. Jagadguru Kripaluji Maharaj states:

> *sau bātan kī bāt ek, dharu muralīdhar dhyan,*
> *badhvahu sevā vāsanā, yah sau jñānam jñān*
>
> (*Bhakti Shatak* verse 74)

'Consider this as the most important of a hundred pieces of wisdom. Keep your mind on Shree Krishna and increase your desire to serve Him.'

It is the eternal principle of the universe—in giving we receive. Look at the rivers that flow towards the ocean. The more the people take away their waters, the more they continue to grow in size. Look again at charitable people. The more they donate in charity, the more their wealth continues to grow.

The same principle applies in the realm of God as well. Think not what God can do for you; think what you can do for God. Consecrate your activities as an act of service to the Supreme. Then, by His grace, you will experience the highest bliss that can be attained by the soul in all creation.

Summary

- The bliss of the formless is called *Brahmanand*, while that of His personal form is called *Premanand*.

- *Premanand*, or divine love bliss, is innumerable times sweeter than *Brahmanand*.

- Saints such as the four Kumars, Janak, Shukadev and Uddhav had attained Brahman realization. Yet, on experiencing a drop of the bliss of the personal form of God, they were naturally drawn towards it.

- God can be realized at different levels of closeness—as Brahman, Paramatma and Bhagavan.

- As Brahman, He pervades all of creation. He is formless, without attributes, and can be compared to divine light.

- Paramatma is the manifestation of God which is seated in everyone's hearts and keeps account of all our karmas.

- Bhagavan is the aspect of God which not only descends in the personal form as an Avatar but also resides eternally in His divine abodes. As Bhagavan, He manifests all His energies. This is the closest realization of the Supreme.

- As we progress on the path of bhakti, at one stage even the desire for happiness gets rejected. It is replaced with a yearning for the happiness of God.

- When we sacrifice our desire for happiness and love God selflessly, we experience the highest bliss.

Glossary

advait	non-dualist philosophy
apauruṣheya	not of human creation
atmāhutī	see *atma samarpaṇ*
atma samarpaṇ	offering one's soul to God
Avatar	descension of God or His special powers on earth
baba	renunciate
Bhagavan	Supreme Lord, who is the possessor of infinite opulences
bhakti	devotion to God
brahma jnani	one who has knowledge of the Supreme
Brahman	formless aspect of God, which is without Names, Virtues, Pastimes
Brahmanand	bliss of the formless aspect of God
chakor	mythical bird
chintan	contemplation; to repeatedly revise a piece of knowledge in the mind and intellect
Darshan Shastras	holy books that enable us to truly see; another name for the Vedic scriptures

Devatā	celestial god
dwait	dualist philosophy
eudaimonia	refers to well-being associated with pursuing meaningful goals that provide a sense of fulfilment
gopis	village maidens who resided in Braj when Shree Krishna displayed His leelas there 5000 years ago
gunas	modes of nature
Guru	God-realized teacher of spirituality
hedonistic	tendency to go for the 'feel good' activities that provide short bursts of delight
janama kundali	natal birth chart
jyotashi	astrologer
karm yog	practice of uniting the mind with God even while doing one's obligatory duties in the world
maha pralaya	the great cosmic dissolution at the end of Brahma's life, wherein the entire creation merges back into Maha Vishnu's body
mahavakyās	four Vedic aphorisms highly emphasized on the path of jnana yog
maya	material energy from which this world is created. It also puts souls, who are forgetful of God,

	into illusion, and makes them transmigrate in the cycle of life and death
mayadhīn	souls that are in a materially bound state
mithyā	illusory and unreal; non-existent
nirguna	not possessing material qualities
nirvikalpa samadhi	state of samadhi characterized by thoughtlessness
parā bhakti	Divine Love
Paramatma	aspect of the Lord as the Supreme Soul residing in all living beings
Paramhansa	elevated soul who effortlessly sees only God everywhere
Premanand	bliss of God's personal form
preya	happiness which is sweet at first but turns into poison later
rajas	see *rajo guna*
rajo guna	mode of passion
samsara	cycle of life and death
sanskārs	tendencies from past lives
sat-chit-anand	eternality, sentience and bliss
sattva	see *sattva guna*
sattva guna	mode of goodness
sattvic	see *sattva guna*

śhreya	happiness that is bitter initially but becomes sweet later
śhruti	knowledge received through the oral tradition; used as another name for the Vedas
tamas	see *tamo guna*
tamo guna	mode of ignorance
Vaikunth	abode of Lord Vishnu in the spiritual realm, beyond the material realm
videha	one who has no perception of his body
vimukhata	consciousness turned away from God
viparyaya	reversal of knowledge under material illusion

Guide to Hindi Pronunciation

Vowels

अ	*a*	as *u* in 'but'
आ	*ā*	as *a* in 'far'
इ	*i*	as *i* in 'pin'
ई	*ī*	as *i* in 'machine'
उ	*u*	as *u* in 'push'
ऊ	*ū*	as *o* in 'move'
ए	*e*	as *a* in 'evade'
ऐ	*ai*	as *a* in 'mat'; sometimes as *ai* in 'aisle' with the only difference that *a* should be pronounced as *u* in 'but', not as *a* in 'far'
ओ	*o*	as *o* in 'go'
औ	*au*	as *o* in 'pot' or as *aw* in 'saw'
ऋ	*ṛi*	as *ri* in 'Krishna'[1]
ॠ	*ṝ*	as *ree* in 'spree'

Consonants

Gutturals: Pronounced from the throat

क	*ka*	as *k* in 'kite'
ख	*kha*	as *kh* in 'Eckhart'

---

[1] Across many states of India, *ṛi* is pronounced as *ru* as *u* in push. In most parts of North India, *ṛi* is pronounced as *ri* in Krishna. We have used the North Indian style here.

ग	*ga*	as *g* in 'goat'
घ	*gha*	as *gh* in 'dighard'
ङ	*ṅa*	as *n* in 'finger'

Palatals: Pronounced with the middle of the tongue against the palate

च	*cha*	as *ch* in 'channel'
छ	*chha*	as *chh* in 'staunchheart'
ज	*ja*	as *j* in 'jar'
झ	*jha*	as *dgeh* in 'hedgehog'
ञ	*ña*	as *n* in 'lunch'

Cerebrals: Pronounced with the tip of the tongue against the palate

ट	*ta*	as *t* in 'tub'
ठ	*ṭha*	as *th* in 'hothead'
ड	*ḍa*	as *d* in 'divine'
ढ	*ḍha*	as *dh* in 'redhead'
ण	*ṇa*	as *n* in 'burnt'

Dentals: Pronounced like the cerebrals but with the tongue against the teeth

त	*ta*	as *t* in French word 'matron'
थ	*tha*	as *th* in 'ether'
द	*da*	as *th* in 'either'
ध	*dha*	as *dh* in 'Buddha'
न	*na*	as *n* in 'no'

Labials: Pronounced with the lips

प	*pa*	as *p* in 'pink'
फ	*pha*	as *ph* in 'uphill'
ब	*ba*	as *b* in 'boy'
भ	*bha*	as *bh* in 'abhor'
म	*ma*	as *m* in 'man'

Semivowels

य	*ya*	as *y* in 'yes'
र	*ra*	as *r* in 'remember'
ल	*la*	as *l* in 'light'
व	*va*	as *v* in 'vine', as *w* in 'swan'

Sibilants

श	*śha*	as *sh* in 'shape'
ष	*ṣha*	as *sh* in 'show'
स	*sa*	as *s* in 'sin'

Aspirate

ह	*ha*	as *h* in 'hut'

Visarga

:	*ḥ*	it is a strong aspirate; also lengthens the preceding vowel and occurs only at the end of a word. It is pronounced as a final *h* sound

Anusvara Nasalized

| | ṁ/ṅ | nasalizes and lengthens the preceding vowel and is pronounced as *n* in the words 'and' or 'anthem'[2] |
| | ~ | as *n* in 'gung-ho' |

Avagraha

| ऽ | ' | This is a silent character indicating अ. It is written but not pronounced; used in specific combination (sandhi) rules |

Others

क्ष	*kṣha*	as *ksh* in 'freakshow'
ज्ञ	*jña*	as *gy* in 'bigyoung'
ड़	*ṛa*	There is no sign in English to represent the sound ड़. It has been written as *ṛa* but the tip of the tongue quickly flaps down
ढ़	*ṛha*	There is no sign in English to represent the sound ढ़. It has been written as *ṛha* but the tip of the tongue quickly flaps down

---

[2] Sometimes nasalized and sometimes not. Many words such as *aṁsh*, *saṁskar*, etc. are pronounced with a nasal sound as *aṅsh*, *saṅskar*, etc. OR Since it is nasalized, we are using *ṅ*.

Other Books by the Author

7 Divine Laws to Awaken Your Best Self
(Also available in Hindi)

7 Mindsets for Success, Happiness and Fulfilment
(Also available in Gujarati, Hindi, Marathi, Oriya, Telugu)

Bhagavad Gita, Song of God

Golden Rules for Living Your Best Life

Science of Healthy Diet

Science of Mind Management
(Also available in Gujarati and Telugu)

Spiritual Dialectics

The Power of Thoughts

Yoga for Body, Mind and Soul

Books for Children

Essence of Hinduism

Festivals of India

Healthy Body, Healthy Mind: Yoga for Children

Inspiring Stories for Children, Vol 1–4

Mahabharat

My Best Friend Krishna

My Wisdom Book: Everyday Shlokas, Mantras, Bhajans and More

Ramayan

Saints of India

Let's Connect

If you enjoyed reading this book and would like to connect with Swami Mukundananda, you can reach him through any of the following channels:

Websites: *www.jkyog.org, www.jkyog.in, www.swamimukundananda.org*

YouTube channels: 'Swami Mukundananda' and 'Swami Mukundananda Hindi'

Facebook: 'Swami Mukundananda' and 'Swami Mukundananda Hindi'

Instagram: 'Swami Mukundananda' and 'Swami Mukundananda Hindi'

LinkedIn: Swami Mukundananda

Pinterest: Swami Mukundananda - JKYog

Telegram: Swami Mukundananda

Twitter: Swami Mukundananda (@Sw_Mukundananda)

Podcasts: Apple, Google, SoundCloud, Spotify, Stitcher

JKYog Radio: TuneIn app for iOS and Android

JKYog App: Available for iOS and Android

WhatsApp Daily Inspirations: We have two broadcast lists. You are welcome to join either or both.

India: +91 84489 41008

USA: +1 346-239-9675

Online Classes:

JKYog India: *www.jkyog.in/online-sessions/*

JKYog US: *www.jkyog.org/online-classes*

Email: deskofswamiji@swamimukundananda.org

To bring *The Art and Science of Happiness* or Swami Mukundananda to your organization—as Google, Intel, Oracle, Verizon, United Nations, Stanford University, Yale University, IITs and IIMs have done—look us up at sm-leadership.org or write to us at mailto:info@sm-leadership.org.